本书配套资源

📂 读者学习资源

1. 技能实训听力文本

本文档为技能实训 4～技能实训 35 "Listening Practice 听力实训"的文本，供读者做完听力练习之后进行核对和学习。

2. 中餐特色菜肴（中英文对照）

3. 饭店场景英文电影片段

为方便读者了解地道的饭店英语使用情境，本书作者剪辑了一些与饭店业相关的经典电影片段，供读者在课余进行观摩学习。

读者扫描右侧二维码，即可获取上述资源。

一书一码，相关资源仅供一人使用。

饭店英语服务实训
（第三版）
请刮开后扫描获取本书资源
本码2028年12月31日前有效

📂 教师教学资源

本书配有教学课件，如任课老师需要，可扫描右边二维码，关注北京大学出版社微信公众号"未名创新大学堂"（zyjy-pku）索取。

- 课件申请
- 样书申请
- 教学服务
- 编读往来

"十二五"职业教育国家规划教材
经全国职业教育教材审定委员会审定

浙江省高职高专"十一五"规划重点建设教材

21世纪职业教育规划教材·旅游系列

饭店英语服务实训

（第三版）

主　编　柯淑萍
副主编　王　君　张丽琴
参　编　柳文娟　余　超

北京大学出版社
PEKING UNIVERSITY PRESS

内 容 简 介

本书以岗位实训和服务流程为主线,内容全面,富有时代感,具有鲜明的特色:① 着眼以岗位服务为模块,具体服务为技能,服务流程为主线的编写模式;② 创建以实训模块为中心的教学模式,以职业技能为中心的互动式教学;③ 实现岗位实训和就业"零距离";④ 培养用英语进行个性化服务和创新工作的能力。

本书可以作为高等职业院校酒店管理等专业的教材,也可作为高星级酒店的培训教材或酒店从业人员自学用书。

图书在版编目(CIP)数据

饭店英语服务实训/柯淑萍主编. —3 版. —北京:北京大学出版社,2023.8
21 世纪职业教育规划教材·旅游系列
ISBN 978-7-301-33562-8

Ⅰ.①饭… Ⅱ.①柯… Ⅲ.①饭店–英语–高等职业教育–教材 Ⅳ.①F719.2

中国版本图书馆 CIP 数据核字(2022)第 201674 号

书　　　名	饭店英语服务实训(第三版) FANDIAN YINGYU FUWU SHIXUN(DI-SAN BAN)
著作责任者	柯淑萍　主编
策 划 编 辑	李　玥
责 任 编 辑	李　玥
标 准 书 号	ISBN 978-7-301-33562-8
出 版 发 行	北京大学出版社
地　　　址	北京市海淀区成府路 205 号　100871
网　　　址	http://www.pup.cn　新浪微博:@北京大学出版社
电 子 信 箱	zpup@pup.cn
电　　　话	邮购部 010-62752015　发行部 010-62750672　编辑部 010-62704142
印 刷 者	北京市科星印刷有限责任公司
经 销 者	新华书店
	787 毫米×1092 毫米　16 开本　16.5 印张　405 千字 2010 年 9 月第 1 版　2016 年 6 月第 2 版 2023 年 8 月第 3 版　2023 年 8 月第 1 次印刷　总第 7 次印刷
定　　　价	49.00 元

未经许可,不得以任何方式复制或抄袭本书之部分或全部内容。
版权所有,侵权必究
举报电话:010-62752024　电子信箱:fd@pup.pku.edu.cn
图书如有印装质量问题,请与出版部联系,电话:010-62756370

前　言

旅游业与酒店业是我国经济发展的支柱产业之一，面对广阔的市场前景，如何培养出相应的人才以满足巨大的需求，是人们关注的热点问题。酒店管理与服务专业旨在培养既具有较强的外语沟通能力，又熟知酒店服务流程并具备专业技能的酒店管理人员和服务人员。

"饭店英语"是高等职业院校酒店管理专业的一门重要的专业必修课，对英语口语和听力有较高的要求，对专业技能的训练也十分注重。因此，在上一版的基础上，编者根据行业发展和市场需求再次修订了《饭店英语服务实训》一书，使其内容全面，更富有时代感。本书以岗位实训和服务流程为主线，每个实训模块提供了大量的专业词汇和语音训练，经典对话全部模拟真实的饭店情景，具有很强的操作性；书中带有🔊标志的部分都配有由外籍专家朗读的音频，读者可扫描每个技能实训中的二维码获取。

本次修订在保持上一版教材核心结构不变的基础上，融入了党的"二十大"精神，对实训模块进行了优化，把"技能实训听力文本""中餐特色菜肴"放入文前二维码中以节省版面；同时，根据《旅游业基础术语》（GB/T 16766—2017）对书中相关术语进行了规范统一，并修改了部分语句，在编写模式上进行了精心设计，具有一定的创新性：

（1）以岗位服务为模块，以具体服务为技能，以服务流程为主线，提高学生饭店岗位英语实用服务技能。

（2）"岗位基础知识"包含 Word Stock（词库）和 Pronunciation（语音训练）两个部分。Word Stock 是对该技能训练模块的一次整理，把跟该训练模块相关的词汇全部罗列出来，扩大学生的词汇量和知识面；而 Pronunciation 中出现的句型都是灵活的，在不同的场合有不同的应对，而且强调发音的准确性与语句的流利性。

（3）"服务流程"包含 Service Performance（服务演练）、Position Practice（岗位实训）、Listening Practice（听力实训）和 Important（特别关注）四个部分。Service Performance 是针对具体技能实训的经典对话；Position Practice 包含了某个技能实训可能出现的各种实训内容，要求学生能够灵活应变，操作性强；Listening Practice 是学生在熟悉实训内容的基础上进一步的岗位演练；Important 是对该模块可能遗漏的一些要点进行补充。

（4）设计了 Case and Development（案例与创新）。Case 要求学生根据该岗位实训的内容进行一次新的演练。Development 中设计的 Topic 不提供现成的答案并且可能有多种答案，要求学生对这些话题进行深入的思考并在自己的岗位上有所创新。

本书由柯淑萍负责模块一至模块四和附录的编写工作，王君负责模块五至模块八的编写工作，张丽琴负责全书的图片拍摄；柳文娟、余超参与了本书的资料收集和整理工作。

本书可以作为高等职业院校酒店管理等专业的教材，也可作为高星级酒店的培训教材或供酒店从业人员自学之用。

编 者
2023 年 6 月

目　录

实训模块一　饭店业须知 Hospitality Industry ABCs ·················· (1)
 技能实训 1　饭店类型 Types of Hotels ·················· (2)
 技能实训 2　服务是什么？What Is Service? ·················· (9)
 技能实训 3　客人类型 Different Guests ·················· (13)

实训模块二　前厅服务 Front Office ·················· (17)
 技能实训 4　客房预订服务 Room Reservation ·················· (18)
 技能实训 5　入住登记服务 Check In ·················· (26)
 技能实训 6　礼宾服务 Concierge ·················· (33)
 技能实训 7　总机服务 Operator ·················· (41)
 技能实训 8　外币兑换服务 Foreign Currency Exchange ·················· (47)
 技能实训 9　结账退房服务 Check Out ·················· (53)
 技能实训 10　商务中心服务 Business Center ·················· (60)

实训模块三　客房服务 Housekeeping ·················· (67)
 技能实训 11　打扫房间 Room Cleaning ·················· (68)
 技能实训 12　洗衣服务 Laundry Service ·················· (75)
 技能实训 13　客房送餐服务 Room Service ·················· (83)
 技能实训 14　维修服务 Maintenance Service ·················· (89)

实训模块四　餐饮服务 Food and Beverage ·················· (95)
 技能实训 15　餐台预订 Reservations ·················· (96)
 技能实训 16　餐厅迎客服务 Receiving Diners ·················· (103)
 技能实训 17　中餐厅服务 At a Chinese Restaurant ·················· (109)
 技能实训 18　西餐厅服务 At a Western Restaurant ·················· (117)

技能实训 19　早餐服务 Breakfast Service ·· (125)

技能实训 20　酒吧服务 At the Bar ·· (131)

技能实训 21　就餐礼仪 Table Manners ·· (139)

实训模块五　康乐中心 Recreation Center ·· (147)

技能实训 22　健身服务 Gym Service ·· (148)

技能实训 23　美容美发服务 Beauty & Hair Salon ·· (155)

技能实训 24　桑拿服务 Sauna Service ·· (161)

技能实训 25　娱乐服务 Entertainment Service ·· (167)

实训模块六　购物服务 Shopping Service ·· (175)

技能实训 26　旅游纪念品 Souvenir ·· (176)

技能实训 27　当地特产 Local Specialty ·· (183)

实训模块七　会展服务 Convention and Exhibition ·· (189)

技能实训 28　会议服务 Convention Service ·· (190)

技能实训 29　展览服务 Exhibition Service ·· (197)

实训模块八　投诉 Complaints ·· (203)

技能实训 30　处理投诉 Dealing with Complaints ·· (204)

技能实训 31　刁钻客人 Difficult Guests ·· (211)

实训模块九　其他服务 Other Services ·· (217)

技能实训 32　失物招领服务 Lost and Found ·· (218)

技能实训 33　寄存服务 Deposit Service ·· (225)

技能实训 34　介绍旅游信息 Tourism Information ·· (231)

技能实训 35　托婴服务 Babysitting Service ·· (237)

附录一　饭店日常用语 ·· (243)

附录二　饭店常用告示语 ·· (249)

参考文献 ·· (253)

实训模块一

饭店业须知
Hospitality Industry ABCs

Hospitality industry is part of the travel and tourism industry. The travel and tourism industry are both vast industries and they have one thing in common: providing necessary or desired products and services to the traveler. The word "hospitality" usually refers to services that are related to hotels, restaurants, tourist attractions, clubs and other services.

饭店业是旅行业、旅游业的组成部分。旅行业和旅游业都是庞大行业，两者有一个共同点：给旅游者提供必要或心仪的产品和服务。"饭店业"一词通常是指与酒店、餐馆、旅游景点、俱乐部以及其他相关的服务性工作。

听力音频

技能实训1 饭店类型 Types of Hotels

Section A

Basic Knowledge for Position 岗位基础知识

I. Word Stock 词库

business hotel	商务饭店
resort hotel	度假饭店
convention hotel	会议饭店
motel	汽车旅馆
apartment hotel	公寓式饭店
airport hotel	机场饭店
budget hotel / economy hotel	经济型饭店
Park Hyatt	柏悦酒店
Banyan Tree Hangzhou	杭州西溪悦榕庄
Pins De La Brume Hotel	九里云松度假酒店
Shangri-la Hotel	香格里拉饭店
Hyatt Regency Hotel	凯悦酒店
Hilton Hotel	希尔顿酒店
Marriott Hotel	万豪酒店
West Lake State Guesthouse	西湖国宾馆
Radisson Plaza Hotel	雷迪森广场酒店
Zhejiang Narada Grand Hotel	浙江世贸君澜大饭店
Merchant Marco Garden Hotel	马可波罗花园酒店
Hangzhou Sunny Hotel	杭州香溢大酒店
Haihua Hotel	海华大酒店
Wuyang Hotel	五洋宾馆
Lakeview Hotel	望湖宾馆
Zhejiang International Hotel	浙江国际大酒店
Super 8 Hotel	速8酒店

Home Inn	如家酒店
Jinjiang Inn	锦江之星
Hanting Hotel	汉庭酒店
Motel 168	莫泰 168
Pod Inn	布丁酒店

 Ⅱ. Pronunciation 语音训练

1. A hotel is a home away from home.
   饭店是家外之家。
2. A hotel is a place that provides temporary and paid accomodation.
   饭店是一个需要付费的临时住所。
3. Reputation first, customer foremost.
   信誉第一，顾客至上。
4. New concepts in hotel design have been developed to meet the needs of guests.
   为了满足客人的需要，饭店在设计上已经融入了新的理念。
5. In a hotel, we can meet and serve people from all walks of life.
   在饭店，我们会遇见各个领域的人并为他们提供服务。
6. Hospitality industry is one branch of service industry. Once you decide to work in service industry, you are obliged to provide more and better service.
   饭店业是服务业的一个分支，你一旦选择了它就意味着要提供更多、更好的服务。

Section B

Position Practice 岗位实训

Hotel ratings according to functions 饭店根据功能划分

1. Business Hotel（商务饭店）

Business hotels provide services for business guests as well as guests that need temporary accomodation. Usually they are located in business center or downtown areas.

商务饭店给商务客人和临时需要住宿的客人提供服务。它们一般位于商务中心或市中心。

2. Motel（汽车旅馆）

The biggest difference between a motel and a general hotel is that the parking space provided by the motel is connected to the room. The first floor is used as a garage and the second floor is a room. This is a typical design for a motel room.

汽车旅馆与一般旅馆最大的不同点，在于汽车旅馆提供的停车位与房间相连。一楼作为车库，二楼为房间，这是汽车旅馆房间的典型设计。

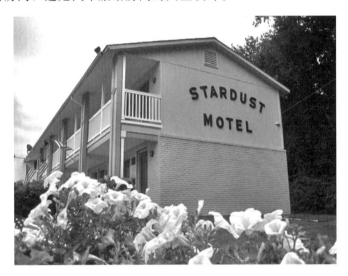

3. Apartment Hotel（公寓式饭店）

An apartment hotel has the layout of home and good living functions, with living room, bedroom, kitchen, and bathroom. It is equipped with a full set of furniture and appliances which can provide guests with professional services of the hotel.

公寓式饭店有居家的格局和良好的居住功能，设有客厅、卧室、厨房和卫生间。它配有全套家具与家电，能够为客人提供饭店的专业服务。

4. Airport Hotel（机场饭店）

Airport hotels are popular because they are always located near major tourist centers. Compared with other types of hotels, airport hotels vary in size and service level. Airport hotels mainly provide service for business guests, passengers or flight attendants whose flight was delayed or cancelled. Hotel-owned buses are used to transport guests to and from the airport.

机场饭店很受欢迎，因为它们通常位于旅游中心附近。与其他类型的饭店相比，机场饭店在规模和服务水平上有很大的不同。机场饭店的客人主要包括商务客人、航班延误或航班取消的乘客和空乘人员。饭店的大巴可以直接接送乘客往返机场。

5. Resort Hotel（度假饭店）

Unlike other types of hotels, resort hotels are the destination of guests. Guests often go on vacation at a resort hotel. Resort hotels often provide scenery and activities that most of the other hotels aren't able to provide. Resort hotel's guests usually stay longer than guests at most of the other types of hotels.

跟其他类型的饭店不同的是，度假饭店就是客人的目的地。客人就在度假饭店里度假。度假饭店提供的景观和活动是其他大部分饭店无法提供的。度假饭店的客人通常比其他类型的饭店客人逗留的时间更长。

6. Conference Hotel（会议饭店）

Different from business hotels that receive business travelers, conference hotels refer to hotels with strong conference functions. Conference hotels generally have a large number of rooms, and the number of accommodations should also match the number of people accommodated in the largest conference room.

与接待商务散客的商务饭店不同，会议饭店是指会议功能比较强的饭店。会议饭店的客房数一般比较多，可接纳的住宿人数一般要与其最大会议室容纳人数相匹配。

7. Budget Hotel/Economy Hotel（经济型饭店）

Budget hotel is the representative of a new value. Budget hotel doesn't equal to the cheap hotel. It includes several basic elements such as the function, price, standard and service. It is a living place where standard services and bearable prices are provided to the common people.

经济型饭店是一种新理念的代表，它并不等同于廉价饭店。它包含几个基本的要素，如功能、价格、水准和服务，可为普通人群提供价格合理、服务标准化的居住场所。

Hotel ratings according to stars 饭店根据星级划分

The star classification system is common in rating hotels. Higher star ratings indicate more luxury service. Factors like food services, entertainments, view, room size, additional amenities, spas and fitness centers, accessibility and location may be considered in hotel ratings.

星级划分系统是比较常见的评价饭店的系统。高星级代表奢华的服务。饮食服务、娱乐、景观、房间规模、附加设施、水疗和健身中心、交通和饭店的位置等因素在评星的时候都会被考虑到。

1-Star hotel provides a limited range of amenities and services, but adheres to a high standard of cleanliness.

一星级饭店提供有限的设施和服务,但遵循较高的清洁标准。

2-Star hotel provides relatively better accommodation and equipped bedrooms, each with a telephone and a private bathroom.

二星级饭店提供的住宿条件相对要好点,每个房间都有电话和单独的卫生间。

3-Star hotel has more spacious rooms, with higher standard of decorations and amenities. It also offers a bar or lounge.

三星级饭店的客房空间更大,装修和设施的标准也更高,还有酒吧间或休息间。

4-Star hotel is much more comfortable and luxurious, and provides excellent cuisine, room service, and other amenities.

四星级饭店更加舒适豪华,提供极好的膳食服务、送餐服务和其他设施。

5-Star hotel offers the most luxurious amenities, widest range of guest services, as well as swimming pool, sports facility and fitness center.

五星级饭店提供十分豪华的设施以及齐全的客户服务,还有游泳池、运动场所和健身中心。

7-Star hotel is like Burj Al Arab in Dubai. Seven star hotels are largely built as marketing tool, since the hotels hope to attract visitors from around the world.

七星级饭店就如迪拜的阿拉伯塔酒店。七星级饭店主要是作为一种营销工具而建造,因为酒店旨在吸引全世界的游客。

Section C
Case and Development 案例与创新

Case 案例

You and your partner both have dreams about career in your minds. Discuss with your partner how to make it come true. Do not be afraid to set your goals high. Do not be afraid to be laughed by others. Do not be so concerned with what you cannot do now but, rather, with what you want to do now. Keep in mind that it is possible to realize your dreams if you have faith and luck.

Development 创新

• Discuss as many types of hotels in your city as possible and discuss their differences in terms of functions.

• Do you have any experience of staying in a hotel? What do you think are the most attractive features of a hotel?

• Is hospitality industry a promising industry in the future? And what will the future hotels be like?

技能实训 2 服务是什么？ What Is Service?

听力音频

Section A

Basic Knowledge for Position 岗位基础知识

I. Word Stock 词库

concierge	门房；礼宾部
golden key	金钥匙
tact	老练，得体
courtesy	礼貌，谦恭，彬彬有礼
endurance	忍耐力，耐久力
punctuality	严守时间；敏捷，守信用
discretion	慎重，谨慎
loyalty	忠诚
honesty	诚实
excellent memory	出色的记忆力
organizing ability	组织能力
language talent	语言才能
flexible	灵活的

Ⅱ. Pronunciation 语音训练

1. I have a real liking for guests and a warm desire to help them.
   我发自内心地喜欢客人，并想热心地帮助他们。
2. Golden management breeds golden service.
   有一流的管理才会有一流的服务。
3. Service is understanding, anticipating and fulfilling needs of others.
   服务是理解、预判、满足他人需要的过程。
4. Good service is a combination of courtesy and efficiency, which means neither excessive intimacy, nor excessive humbleness.
   好的服务是礼貌和效率的融合，意味着不过度亲近也不过分谦卑。
5. Thanks to our excellent services, the guests are willing to come again.
   因为我们出色的服务，客人很乐意再度光临。

Section B

Position Practice 岗位实训

Ten golden keys for hotel service 饭店服务的十把金钥匙

1. The customer is God.
   顾客是上帝。
2. Talk with guests.
   跟客人交谈。
3. Smile at people.
   对他人微笑。
4. Be sincere, honest and friendly.
   真诚，诚实，友好。
5. Call guests by name.
   称呼客人的名字。
6. Be helpful.
   为客人提供帮助。
7. Wear your name badge.
   戴上你的胸牌。

8. Take pride in your image.
   对自己的形象有信心。
9. Consider the feelings of others.
   能够体谅别人的感受。
10. Know your job and your hotel.
    了解你的工作和你的酒店。

What does SERVICE represent 服务代表什么

S——smiles（向每个人微笑）
E——excellence in everything we do（对我们所做的每件事都力求完美）
R——reaching out to every guest with hospitality（热情对待每位客人）
V——viewing every guest as special（把每位客人都当作特别的客人）
I——inviting guests to come again（欢迎客人再次光临）
C——creating a warm atmosphere（创造温馨的气氛）
E——eye contact that shows we care（用眼神表示我们的关注）

What is Golden Key / Les Clefs d'Or 什么是金钥匙

The French phrase Les Clefs d'Or means "Golden Keys" in English. Golden Keys are awarded by Union Internationale des Concierges d'Hôtels. This organization is a non-political and non-religious organization, and is definitely not a trade union. It's based on friendship between members to assist international travelers and tourists. A concierge who has the qualification of wearing a golden key is called "Golden Key". She or he will do anything you have asked meticulously as long as it is moral, legal and human. You can actually ask her/him of any types of service and find that all is completed and done to your satisfaction while you are away attending your business appointment or sightseeing. Les Clefs d'Or Concierge is a remarkable man. It took years of hard working and professional training to become it.

法语单词Les Clefs d'Or翻译成英语就是"金钥匙"。"金钥匙"由国际金钥匙组织颁发，这是一家非政治、非宗教、非贸易性质的组织，纯粹是出于组织成员中的友谊来帮助国际旅行者和游客。一个有资格佩戴金钥匙标记的礼宾就被称作"金钥匙"。她/他能为客人提供无微不至的服务，只要是在合理、合法、人性的基础上。您在参加商务活动或旅游观光时可以向她/他提出任何要求，她/他一定能够让您满意。"金钥匙"是极为优秀的员工，要有多年的努力付出和专业培训才可能获得。

Section C

Case and Development 案例与创新

Case 案例

Work with your partner and give the whole class a presentation on why you choose hotel service and management as your major. The following expressions may be helpful for you.

I enjoy dealing with people because …

I like meeting new people.

People are usually very friendly.

I find it challenging.

Every person you meet is different.

I can experience different culture.

Development 创新

- What does teamwork mean?
- What can you do if you wish most guests to be repeat guests in your hotel?
- What requirements are necessary to be a successful staff member in a hotel?

技能实训 3　客人类型 Different Guests

听力音频

Section A

Basic Knowledge for Position 岗位基础知识

Ⅰ. Word Stock 词库

package tour	包价旅行
tour group	旅行队
group code	团号
tour leader	领队
walk-in guest	散客
backpacker	背包客
pleasure travelers	消遣型游客
business travelers	商务型游客
domestic travelers	国内游客
foreign independent travelers (FITs)	国外散客
group inclusive travelers (GITs)	团队全包游客
special interest travelers (SITs)	特殊游客
corporate business travelers	团队商务游客
conference participants	参加会议者
independent traveler	旅游散客
repeat guest	回头客
regular guest	老客户

Ⅱ. Pronunciation 语音训练

1. The more information a hotel collects from its guests, the better it can meet their needs.
   酒店从客人那里得到的信息越多，就越能够满足客人的需求。
2. The guests don't depend on the hotels but the hotels depend on the guests.
   客人不依赖酒店而酒店依赖客人。
3. Pleasure travelers travel for pleasure.
   消遣型游客出行的目的是消遣。
4. Pleasure travelers are generally price sensitive.
   消遣型游客通常对价格比较敏感。

5. Business travelers mainly travel for conducting business.
   商务型游客出行的主要目的是商务活动。
6. Business travelers are the largest source of hotels.
   商务型游客是酒店最主要的客源。
7. Guests desire comfortable, modern surroundings and leisure facilities to relax.
   客人希望拥有舒适、现代的环境和可供放松的娱乐设施。

Section B
Position Practice 岗位实训

Classification of travelers 旅游者的分类

1. Pleasure and business travelers as to the purpose of visit.
   按旅行目的划分,游客可分为消遣型游客和商务型游客。
2. Independent and group travelers as to numbers.
   按人数划分,游客可分为散客和团体游客。
3. Domestic and foreign travelers as to the origin.
   按客源国划分,游客可分为国内游客和国外游客。
4. Package travelers and non-package travelers as to the price.
   按计价方式划分,游客可分为包价游客和非包价游客。
5. Budget travelers, mass travelers and luxury travelers as to the consumption level.
   按消费水平划分,游客可分为经济型游客、大众型游客和豪华型游客。

There is only one boss in the hotel 酒店只有一个老板

★ There is only one boss. The customer! He can fire anybody in the hotel, from General Manager down to the bottom staff simply by spending his money in other hotels!
只有一个老板,那就是顾客!他可以解雇酒店中的任何一个人,从总经理到最下面的员工。只要把他的钱花在其他酒店就可以做到!

★ There is very little difference among people. But that little difference makes BIG difference. The little difference is ATTITUDE. The BIG difference is whether it is POSITIVE or NEGATIVE!

人与人之间没有太大差别，但是小差别可以造成大不同。小差别是指态度的差别，即态度是积极的还是消极的。

Section C
Case and Development 案例与创新

Case 案例

Imagine that one of you is a foreign guest from Australia. He is a professor teaching Chinese ancient culture in a university. Make a conversation about why he comes to China and what will be interesting to him.

Development 创新

- What are the most important reasons for you to travel?
- What are the advantages and disadvantages of developing tourism in your region?
- How can you be a responsible traveler?

实训模块二

前厅服务
Front Office

The Front Office is the control center of the hotel. Staff at the Front Office must be well trained and motivated in order to achieve business objectives of high yield, high occupancy rates and high quality service. In this unit, we'll practice reservation procedure, list the steps of check in and check out, explain the methods of payments and describe the hotel telephone system, duties of concierge and business service.

前厅部是酒店的管理中心。为了达到高产出、高入住率、高质量的服务目标，前厅部员工应该训练有素、积极主动。本实训模块将训练订房、入住、退房、付款方式、电话、礼宾、商务服务等一系列服务流程。

技能实训4 客房预订服务 Room Reservation

Section A

Basic Knowledge for Position 岗位基础知识

I. Word Stock 词库

single room	单人间
double room	大床间（供夫妇合睡的）
twin room（standard room）	双床间（标准间）
triple room	三人间（配备三张单人床）
quad room	四人间
studio room	工作室型客房
junior suite	普通套房
business suite	商务套房（一间为起居兼办公室，另一间为卧室）
senior suite	高级套房
connecting rooms	组合套房
duplex suite	立体套房（起居室在下，卧室在上）
deluxe suite	豪华套房
presidential suite	总统套房
lake-view room	湖景房
mountain-view room	山景房
queen-size bed	大号双人床
king-size bed	特大号双人床
room charge	房价
group rate	团队价
discount rate	折扣价
package rate	包价
free of charge	免费
recommend	推荐
room availability	客房预订情况（是否有空房间）
reservation record	预订记录
off/low season	淡季
peak/high season	旺季

Ⅱ. Pronunciation 语音训练

1. What type of room would you like?
   您想要什么样的房间？
2. When would you like your room, sir?
   先生，您什么时候入住？
3. How many people is the room for, madam?
   女士，请问房间几个人住？
4. How long do you plan to stay, sir?
   先生，您准备住多久？
5. May I have your name and telephone number, please?
   可以告诉我您的名字和电话号码吗？
6. Could you spell your name for me, please?
   能否请您拼一下您的名字？
7. I'll just check if we have a room available.
   我查一下我们有没有空房。
8. Let me just confirm the details of your reservation, please.
   我来确认一下您的预订信息。
9. The room rate for a standard room is ＄300 per night.
   一个标准间一个晚上的房价是300美元。
10. I'm afraid we have no suite available. Would you mind a double room instead?
    我们恐怕没有空余的套房了。您介意改为大床间吗？
11. It is the peak season. I'm sorry, but could you call us again on weekend? Maybe we'll have some cancellations.
    现在是旺季，非常抱歉，请您周末再打电话过来好吗？可能会有人取消预订。
12. Thank you for calling. We are looking forward to seeing you, madam.
    女士，谢谢您的来电。我们期待您的光临。

Section B

Service Procedure 服务流程

1. Greetings.
   问候。
2. Reservation details: room type and number of people, arrival date and departure date.

订房信息：房型、人数、抵达日期和离店日期。

3. Check the room availability.

   查询客房预订情况。

4. Get the information from the guest: name, telephone number.

   获取客人的个人信息，如名字、电话。

5. Confirm the reservation.

   确认预订。

6. Express your wishes.

   表达你的祝福。

7. Form the reservation record and hand over to the front desk.

   形成预订记录并交给前台。

I. Service Performance 服务演练

G＝Guest（客人）　　　　R＝Reservationist（预订员）

R：Good morning, Radisson Plaza Hotel, Room Reservation. Can I help you?

　　早上好，雷迪森广场酒店客房预订部。需要我为您服务吗？

G：Yes, I'd like to book a room.

　　是的，我想预订一间房。

R：Thank you, sir. For which date and how many people will there be in your party?

　　谢谢您，先生。请问您要哪一天的房？还有你们一共有几个人？

G：From May 1st to May 5th, just me and my son.

　　从5月1日到5月5日，就我和我儿子。

R：From May 1st to May 5th and what kind of room would you like, sir?

　　从5月1日到5月5日，请问您要哪种房型？

G：A suite, please.

　　一间套房吧。

R：A junior suite or a deluxe suite?

　　是普通套房还是豪华套房？

G：What's the difference in price?

　　价格上有什么差别？

R：A junior suite is ＄120 per night and a deluxe one is ＄150 per night. Both include buffet breakfast.

　　普通套房一个晚上120美元，豪华套房一个晚上150美元，两种房型都含自助式早餐。

G：I think I will take a deluxe suite, please.

　　我想我还是订一间豪华套房吧。

R：Hold on please. I'll check the room availability...Thank you for waiting, sir. We do have a deluxe suite at $150 per night, will that be all right?

请别挂断,我查一下是否有空房……谢谢等候,先生。我们能够为您预订一间豪华套房,每晚150美元,您看行吗?

G: OK, I'll take it.

好的,我订下。

R: May I have your name and telephone number, please?

能够告诉我您的名字和电话吗?

G: Sure, my name is Goldfield, Tony Goldfield, and my telephone number is 53638696.

当然,我的名字是戈德菲尔德,托尼·戈德菲尔德,我的电话号码是53638696。

R: Could you spell it, please?

请问怎么拼?

G: G—O—L—D—F—I—E—L—D.

G—O—L—D—F—I—E—L—D。

R: Thank you, Mr. Goldfield. May I know your arrival time, please?

谢谢,戈德菲尔德先生。能够告诉我您的抵达时间吗?

G: At about 5 p.m. on May 1st.

大概在5月1日下午5点。

R: Fine. How would you like to make payment, sir?

好的。您准备用哪种方式付款?

G: Do you accept MasterCard?

你们接受万事达信用卡吗?

R: Yes. May I know the number?

是的,可以告诉我卡号吗?

G: It's 5336876925658721.

卡号是5336876925658721。

R: Thank you, Mr. Goldfield. You'd like to have a deluxe suite from May 1st to May 5th for 4 nights. Thank you for calling and we are looking forward to seeing you soon.

谢谢,戈德菲尔德先生。您预订的是一间从5月1日到5月5日的豪华套房,一共4个晚上。谢谢您的来电,我们期待您的光临。

II. Position Practice 岗位实训

★ Introduce the room type to the guest.(向客人介绍房型)

We have single room, double room, twin room and deluxe suite, which one do you prefer?

我们有单人间、大床间、双床间和豪华套房,您要哪一种?

★ Room types（房型）
1. Single Room（单人间）

Meant for a single occupancy. The room has a single bed.

2. Double Room（大床间）

Meant for double occupancy and has one large bed meant for two.

3. Twin Room（双床间）

Meant for double occupancy. The room provides two single beds.

4. Triple Room（三人间）

Provided mostly for families. It has twin beds with an extra cot.

5. Suite（套房）

Meant for single or more occupancy. It has a living room connected to one or more bedrooms.

6. Deluxe Suite（豪华套房）

Deluxe suite bedrooms are targeted to the most sophisticated group of people.

7. Studio Room（工作室型客房）

Meant for single or double occupancy. It has one single bed and a sofa which acts as a normal sofa during the day and can be pulled out into a bed for the night.

8. Connecting room（连通客房）

Two or more rooms with private connecting doors.

9. Adjoining Room（并联客房）

Two or more rooms side by side with a connecting door among them.

★ Introduce room rate to the guest.（向客人介绍房价）
   The room rate for a junior suite is $150 per night, including buffet breakfast.
   一间普通套房每晚房价是150美元，包含自助早餐。

★ Confirm the reservation.（确认预订）
   So that's a twin room for Mr. Johnson from June 5th to 7th at $120 per night, correct?
   约翰逊先生预订一间从6月5日到7日的双床间，每晚120美元，对吗？

★ Extend the reservation for the guest.（为客人延长预订）
   We'll extend the reservation for you.
   我们将帮您延长预订。

★ Change the reservation for the guest.（帮客人更改预订）
   You'd like to change your double room for a twin room, is that right?
   您想把大床间改成双床间，是吗？

★ Cancel the reservation for the guest.（帮客人取消预订）
   Don't worry, sir. We'll make the cancellation for you.
   不要着急，先生，我们将帮您取消预订。

Ⅲ. Listening Practice 听力实训

★ A. Listen to the conversation and fill in the reservation form.

Zhejiang Narada Grand Hotel
Reservation Form

Mr/Mrs/Miss _____
First Name _____   Last name _____
Check in _____   Check out _____
Room Type _____   Room Rate _____
Tel Number _____
Remarks _____

★ B. Make confirmation about the details of the reservation.

Miss _____, can I repeat the _____ of your reservation? You are reserving a room for Mr. _____, who will be arriving on flight CX 837 at 8 p.m. on _____ and staying until _____. Mr. _____ requires a _____ for _____. The room rate is _____ per night. Your address in Singapore is _____, and your telephone number is _____, is that right?

Important 特别关注

▲ Never deny a reservation without offering an optional date, room type or hotel.
婉拒订房时应提供可选择的日期、房型或饭店。
▲ Record the reason for denial.
记录婉拒订房的原因。
▲ All changes must be put on record.
所有的预订变化都应记录在案。
▲ All information must be promptly updated in the Front Office system.
所有的信息应该在前厅的系统中及时得到更新。

Section C

Case and Development 案例与创新

Case 案例

You are a clerk in Room Reservation in Marriott Hotel. Mr. Brown wants to book five twin rooms and two suites for his company from July 10th to 12th. But it's high season, you can only offer three twin rooms, two double rooms and two suites. You answer the phone and confirm the reservation details.

Development 创新

- If there are no rooms available in your hotel, what will you do for the guests?
- If you are a clerk in Room Reservation, how will you confirm a cancellation?
- What kind of reservation do you think would be popular in the future? Why?

技能实训 5　入住登记服务 Check In

Section A
Basic Knowledge for Position 岗位基础知识

Ⅰ. Word Stock 词库

lobby	大堂
black list	黑名单
check in	登记入住
ID card	身份证
passport	护照
service charge	服务费
deposit	押金
arrival list	预期抵店客人名单
departure list	离店客人名单
room card	房卡
date of departure	离店日期
breakfast coupon	早餐券
reconfirm	重新确认
surname	姓
first name	名字
nationality	国籍
signature	签名
corridor	走廊
elevator	电梯
procedure	过程，步骤，程序
registration	登记，注册
occupied room	已住客房
check-out room	走客房
reserved room	预留房

Ⅱ. Pronunciation 语音训练

1. Do you have a reservation?
   您有预订吗？
2. How long will you stay, please?
   您准备住多久？
3. How would you like to pay, please?
   请问您用什么方式付款？
4. Could you sign your name here, please?
   您能在这儿签名吗？
5. May I see your passport?
   可以看一下您的护照吗？
6. Do you have an e-mail confirmation of your reservation?
   您有预订的邮件确认吗？
7. Could you fill in this registration form?
   您能填一下入住登记表吗？
8. Please don't forget to keep your room card with you.
   请您不要忘记随身携带房卡。
9. Your room is on the 16th floor, the room number is 1615.
   您的房间在16楼，房号是1615。
10. If you are ready, I'll ask the bellman to show you to your room.
    如果您一切就绪，我叫行李员带您去房间。

Section B

Service Procedure 服务流程

1. Greetings.
   问候。
2. Identify reservation status.
   确认客人是否有预订。
3. Record registration information.
   记录入住登记信息。
4. Assign rooms and charge.
   分配房间和收费。

5. Confirm ways of payment.
   确认付款方式。
6. Go through registration procedure.
   完成入住登记手续。
7. Document all the information.
   建立相关资料信息。

Ⅰ. Service Performance 服务演练

G＝Guest（客人）　　　　R＝Receptionist（接待员）

R：Good evening. Welcome to Holiday Inn. Can I help you?
　　晚上好，欢迎光临假日酒店。需要为您服务吗？

G：Good evening. I'd like to check in please.
　　晚上好！我想登记入住。

R：Have you made a reservation, Miss?
　　小姐，请问您有预订吗？

G：I'm afraid I don't have a reservation. Is there a vacant room here?
　　我没有预订，还有空房吗？

R：Just a moment please… Sorry to have you wait, Miss. We still have some vacant rooms. What do you want, a single or a double room?
　　请稍等片刻……很抱歉让您久等了，小姐。我们还有一些空房。您需要单人间还是大床间？

G：A single please. How much does it cost?
　　单人间就可以了。单人间的房价是多少钱？

R：It's ＄100 per night for a single room.
　　单人间每晚100美元。

G：Can you give me some discount?
　　能够打折吗？

R：Yes, we give 5％ discount for one week, 10％ for two weeks and over. How long do you intend to stay?
　　可以，如果住一周我们给您打九五折，如果住两周或更长时间我们给您打九折。您准备住多久呢？

G：For a week.
　　住一周。

R：Then we can give you 5％ discount.
　　这样我们可以给您打九五折。

G：All right. I'll take the room for a week.
　　好吧，我要一间房住一周。

R: Could you fill out the registration form, please?
请您填写一下入住登记表好吗？

G: Fine.
好的。

R: How would you like to pay, Miss?
小姐，您准备用哪种方式付款？

G: By Visa Card.
用维萨卡付款。

R: May I take a print of your card?
能够刷一下您的信用卡吗？

G: Sure, here you are.
当然，给你。

R: Thank you, Miss Julie. Your room number is 1211. A bellboy will show you to your room. Enjoy your stay here, please.
谢谢您，茱莉小姐。您的房号是1211。行李员会带您去房间。祝您在这儿过得愉快！

Ⅱ. Position Practice 岗位实训

★ Identify guest's reservation status. （确认客人的预订情况）

1. Do you have a reservation with us, sir?
   先生，您有预订吗？
2. Have you made a reservation, madam?
   女士，您有预订吗？
3. May I have your name, please?
   能够告诉我您的名字吗？

★ Walk-in guest check-in. （散客入住）

1. Which type of room do you prefer, sir?
   先生，您要哪种房型？
2. How long do you plan to stay in our hotel, madam?
   女士，您准备住多久？
3. Just a moment, please. I'll check the reservation record.
   请稍等，我查一下预订记录。
4. I'm sorry, sir. There is no single room available, would you like a twin room instead?
   很抱歉，先生，已经没有单人间了，来一间双床间怎么样？

★ Group check-in. （团队入住）

1. Pre-allocate vacant rooms to the group's requirements.

按照团队的要求预先分配好房间。

2. Input group reservation into group check-in screen.
   在团队入住屏幕中输入团队预订。

3. First check-in members of group, then check-in all pre-allocated rooms.
   先登记团队的人员，然后登记预先分配好的房间号码。

4. Input group details into the computer and print list of room numbers, Concierge and Front Office shall have a copy.
   把团队的详细信息输入电脑并复印房号名单，礼宾部和前厅部各持一份名单。

5. Record all room numbers.
   记录所有的房号。

6. Attach a room number to each room card.
   每张房卡上都应该有房号。

7. Greet guests friendly.
   用礼貌的方式问候客人。

8. Give all room cards to the group leader, and indicate the locations.
   所有的房卡都交给领队，并说明房间的位置。

9. Offer guests assistance with luggage.
   为客人提供行李服务。

Ⅲ. Listening Practice 听力实训

★ A. Listen to the conversation and fill in the registration form.

Registration Form

Mr/Mrs/Miss _____

Surname _____　　　　Fist Name _____

Check in _____

Check out _____

Room No. _____　　　　Room charge _____

From _____　　　　To _____

Nationality _____　　　　Passport No. _____

Home Address _____

Purpose of Stay _____

Payment by Cash/Credit Card/Traveler's Check/Company Check

Guest Signature _____

★ B. Complete the following dialogue.

Guest: Good evening, my name is Thompson. I've just arrived from New York. I had a reservation.

Receptionist: Welcome to Marriot Hotel, Mrs. Thompson.

Guest: Thank you.

Receptionist: Just a minute, please. I'll check the reservation for you. _____. Are you traveling with your family?

Guest: No, I'm here on business.

Receptionist: I see. So _____, do you?

Guest: No, of course. My secretary booked _____.

Receptionist: I see. Well, I'm afraid we have made a mistake about the reservation. I do apologize for it. _____?

Guest: Yes, just one moment. Here it is— "one deluxe single" for five nights. That's until 15th.

Receptionist: Um… Yes, I see. Well, _____ while I find out if there are any deluxe singles still available?

Guest: Very well, I hope this won't happen again.

Important 特别关注

▲ Immediately greet an arriving guest, regardless of what you are doing at that time.
无论你正在做什么,一定要立刻接待抵达的客人。

▲ Use proper greetings, do not simply nod or raise your head.
使用恰当的问候,而不只是点头或抬头。

▲ Offer to help rather than let a guest wait.
主动提供帮助而不是让客人等候。

▲ Regardless of what the Front Office receptionist is doing, he must always pay attention to an arriving guest. When talking on the telephone (a business call of course), the receptionist must tell the person on the phone to hold the line, greet the guest using a sentence like: "Good afternoon, I will be with you in a few moment," then return to the person on the phone and end the conversation as soon as possible. If the receptionist is unable to end the conversation quickly, he must ask a colleague either to answer the telephone or to greet the arriving guest.
无论前厅接待员在做什么,他必须时刻关注到来的客人。如果他正在接听电话(当然是商务电话),他必须告诉听电话的一方稍等,向到来的客人打招呼:"下午好,我马上就好了。"然后转向听电话的一方并尽快结束电话。如果无法很快结束电话,他必须叫他的同事来接听电话或接待到来的客人。

Section C

Case and Development 案例与创新

Case 案例

The guest's name is Tony Waller. He would like to have a twin room for tonight but he didn't make a reservation in advance.

You are a receptionist. You check the reservation record and find there is no twin room, you suggest a double room for the guest. Then you ask the guest to fill in the registration form. The room charge is 680 yuan. The room number is 608. The bellboy will show the guest to the room.

Development 创新

• What are the main points the receptionist has to tell group guests? Try to list them in your own words.

• If the guest wants to change the room, what will you do?

• As a hotel receptionist, what personal qualities and skills should you possess?

技能实训 6 礼宾服务 Concierge

听力音频

Section A

Basic Knowledge for Position 岗位基础知识

I. Word Stock 词库

bellman	行李员
door man	门童
bell captain	行李领班
luggage tag	行李标签
luggage cart	行李车
luggage rack	行李架
luggage deposit	行李存放处
claim tag	取物牌
cloakroom	寄存处
flight number	航班号
pick-up service	接机服务
shuttle service	接送服务；班车服务
automobile	小汽车
shuttle bus	穿梭巴士
group baggage registration	团队行李登记
rooming list	分房单
parking	停车场
fitness club	健身俱乐部
entertainment center	娱乐中心
beauty salon	美容室

II. Pronunciation 语音训练

1. May I help you with your luggage, sir?
   先生，我来帮您提行李好吗？

2. May I take them for you?
   我来帮您提行李好吗?

3. Is this all your luggage?
   这是您所有的行李吗?

4. Everything here, sir?
   这是全部东西吗,先生?

5. You may leave your luggage in the Concierge.
   您可以把行李放在礼宾部。

6. Would you like to deposit your luggage here?
   您要寄存行李吗?

7. Don't worry, your luggage will be sent up soon.
   别担心,您的行李很快就会被送上去的。

8. Your entire luggage is here, seven pieces in all.
   您所有的行李都在这儿,总共7件。

9. How many pieces of luggage do you have?
   您有几件行李?

10. Is there anything valuable or fragile in it?
    请问里面有贵重物品或易碎物品吗?

11. I'll show you to the front desk. This way, please.
    我带您到前台,请这边走。

12. I'll show you to your room. May I have your room number, please?
    我带您去房间,请告诉我您的房号好吗?

13. After you, sir. May I put your suitcases here?
    先生,您先请。我能把行李放在这儿吗?

14. Here we are, sir. Room 1615.
    先生,我们到了,1615房间。

15. May I have your room card?
    能够用一下您的房卡吗?

16. Where shall I put your luggage?
    我把您的行李放在哪儿?

17. Is there anything else I can do for you?
    还有什么需要我效劳的吗?

18. Thank you, sir. You are so kind.
    谢谢您,先生。您真好。

19. Watch your steps, madam.
    女士,小心。

20. Would you like me to call a taxi for you? / Would you want a taxi?
    您需要我为你叫一辆出租车吗？/ 您需要出租车吗？

21. About 30 minutes by taxi from here to the airport.
    从这里到机场大概需要 30 分钟。

22. I'm sorry to have kept you waiting.
    对不起让您久等了。

Section B

Service Procedure 服务流程

1. Greetings.
   问候。

2. Help guests to take luggage out of the taxi.
   帮助客人从出租车上拿出行李。

3. Confirm pieces of luggage.
   确认行李数量。

4. Show the guest to the front desk.
   带客人到前台。

5. Wait for the guest while checking in.
   等候客人登记入住。

6. Show the guest to his room.
   带客人去房间。

7. Open the door.
   开门。

8. Express your wishes to the guest.
   向客人表达祝愿。

Ⅰ. Service Performance 服务演练

G＝Guest（客人）　　　　B＝Bellman（行李员）

B：Welcome to West Lake State Guesthouse.
　　欢迎光临西湖国宾馆。

G：Thank you.
　　谢谢。

B：May I help you with your luggage?

我来帮您提行李好吗？

G：Thank you.

谢谢。

B：How many pieces of luggage do you have?

您有几件行李？

G：Seven pieces in all.

总共7件。

B：But here are just five pieces.

但是这里只有5件。

G：Oh, two pieces are still in the taxi.

哦，还有两件在出租车里。

B：I'll take them for you.

我来帮您拿吧。

G：Thank you.

谢谢。

B：Just a moment, please. I will bring a luggage cart. Now I'll show you to the front desk. This way, please.

请稍等，我去拿一辆行李车。现在我带您去前台，请这边走。

G：Thank you.

谢谢。

B：I'll show you to your room after you finish checking in.

您办完入住登记后，我带您去房间。

G：OK.

好的。

(After a while.)（过了一会儿）

B：Now I'll show you to your room. May I have your room number, please?

现在我带您去房间，请告诉我您的房号好吗？

G：My room number is 1216.

我的房号是1216。

B：This way, please.

请这边走。

G：Thank you.

谢谢。

B：Here we are. Room 1216. May I have your room card, please?

我们到了，1216房间。我可以用一下您的房卡吗？

G：Sure. Here you are.

当然，给你。

B：After you, sir. May I put your suitcases here?
先生，您先请。我能把行李放在这儿吗？

G：Sure. Just put them anywhere.
可以，放在哪里都行。

B：Shall I open the window for you?
需要打开窗户吗？

G：Yes, thank you.
打开吧，谢谢。

B：Is there anything else I can do for you?
还有什么需要我为您服务的吗？

G：No, thank you.
没有了，谢谢。

B：You're welcome. I hope you will enjoy your stay with us.
不用客气。祝您入住愉快！

Ⅱ. Position Practice 岗位实训

★ Confirm the pieces of luggage. （确认行李件数）
1. How many pieces of luggage do you have?
   您有几件行李？
2. Your entire luggage is here, five pieces in all. Let me take them to the trunk.
   您所有的行李都在这儿，一共5件。让我把它们放到后备厢吧。

★ Confirm luggage for group guests. （确认团队客人的行李）
Pay attention to the number of luggage, if it is damaged or undamaged, and the luggage tags.
关注行李的件数、行李是否损坏、行李的标签。

★ Call a taxi for the guest. （为客人叫出租车）
1. Would you like me to call a taxi for you?
   您需要一辆出租车吗？
2. Where to? Sir.
   先生，去哪里呢？
3. Sorry to have kept you waiting, sir.
   先生，不好意思让您久等了。

★ Arrange a city tour for the guest. （为客人安排城市观光）
1. I suggest that you go and visit the West Lake tomorrow. It's a must for tourists in Hangzhou.
   我建议你们明天去逛西湖，对于到杭州的游客来说，西湖是一个必去的地方。
2. You can visit the Oriental Pearl TV Tower. People say it's the symbol of our city.

你们可以去看看东方明珠广播电视塔，大家都说它是这个城市的象征。

3. The Forbidden City is one of the most famous tourist attractions in Beijing. It is the largest and most well reserved imperial palace in China today.

故宫是北京最有名的景点之一，是当今中国最大也是保护得最好的皇宫。

★ At the cloakroom.（行李寄存）

1. Excuse me, where can the bag be deposited?
   对不起，哪里能寄存行李？

2. I want to check my luggage.
   我想要寄存我的行李。

3. You can check luggage here.
   您可以把行李寄存在这里。

4. Certainly, sir. Please go through the deposit formalities.
   先生，当然可以。请您办一下寄存手续。

5. Keep the luggage deposit card, and when you pick up the luggage, please show the second half of this card.
   请保存好行李寄存卡，当您来取回行李时，请出示这张卡的下半联。

Ⅲ. Listening Practice 听力实训

★ A. Listen to the conversation and fill in the baggage form.

Holiday Inn

Baggage Tag Name _____

Room No. _____

Pieces of Baggage _____

Collecting Time _____

Remarks _____

Handled by _____

★ B. Complete the following Dialogue.

Guest: Hi, I was told to see you about _____.

Concierge: It's my pleasure. _____.

Guest: Concierge? Could you explain that to me?

Concierge: We help direct hotel visitors to _____.

Guest: Very good. So where shall I begin my sightseeing?

Concierge: I would suggest that you visit the Forbidden City first.

Guest: Gee, I've already seen the Forbidden City. _____?

Concierge: Let me see. What do you like to do _____?

Guest: Well, I really like climbing mountains.
Concierge: Well, _____! Have you ever visited the Great Wall?
Guest: No, but I've been intended to.
Concierge: Well, the Great Wall _____. It will really impress you.
Guest: _____. I'll do that.
Concierge: Enjoy your visit!

Important 特别关注

▲ Always address a guest by his name.
记得客人的姓名，见面时恰当地打招呼。

▲ Every time you see a guest, smile and offer a friendly greeting.
每次遇见客人都面带微笑，进行友好的寒暄。

▲ Answer the guests' questions and requests quickly and efficiently.
迅速回答客人的问题，高效处理客人的要求。

▲ Anticipate the guests' needs and deal with guests' problems.
预测客人的需求并处理客人的问题。

▲ Let the guest enter the room first.
让客人先进房间。

▲ Show necessary items to the guest but do not over-stay.
给客人介绍必要的设施，但不要待太久。

▲ Bid proper farewell.
恰当地道别。

Section C

Case and Development 案例与创新

Case 案例

Make a dialogue with your partner. You are a concierge. You receive a call from a registered guest named Mr. Thompson. His room number is 1619, he wants to check out and go out for an important appointment in 30 minutes. He has no time to deal with his luggage. He calls you for help. You tell him you will send a bellman immediately to get his luggage. You also ask your guest to put his name tag on the cases. Mr. Thompson asks if it is possible to leave his luggage in the hotel until 3 p.m. You tell him everything will be OK.

Development 创新

• What kind of topic should you avoid when you have a friendly talk with the guests?

• When handling the luggage for group guests, what are the most important points that you should always remember?

• How can you anticipate the guest's need and offer your best service to him?

技能实训 7　总机服务 Operator

听力音频

Section A

Basic Knowledge for Position 岗位基础知识

I. Word Stock 词库

operator	话务员
dial	拨电话
inside call/outside call	内线/外线电话
local call	市内电话
long distance call	长途电话
Domestic Direct Dial call (DDD call)	国内长途直拨
International Direct Dial call (IDD call)	国际长途直拨
area code	区号
country code	国家代码
collect call	对方付费电话
paid call	自己付费电话
coin call	投币电话
emergency call	急救电话
wrong number	打错电话
morning call/wake-up call	叫早电话/叫醒电话
put sb. through	给某人接通电话
minimum charge	最低收费
extension	分机
directory book/telephone book	电话簿
house phone	内部电话
hold on/hold the line	别挂断

II. Pronunciation 语音训练

1. Hello. This is Radisson Plaza Hotel. May I help you?
   您好，雷迪森广场酒店。可以为您做什么？
2. Hello. This is Room Reservation. Can I help you?
   您好，这是客房预订，可以为您做什么？

3. Who is that? / Who is that speaking?
   请问您是哪位?

4. This is Helen. / This is Helen speaking.
   我是海伦。

5. Lily, you are wanted. / Lily, you are wanted on the phone.
   莉莉,你的电话。

6. I'm afraid you have got the wrong number.
   恐怕您打错电话了。

7. Could you put me through to the Front Office?
   可以帮我接通前厅部吗?

8. The line is busy now. Could you call back later?
   电话占线,您要不要过一会儿再打过来?

9. He is not in the room at the moment. Would you like to leave a message?
   他现在不在房间里,您要不要留个口信?

10. You are through, sir. Please go ahead.
    先生,接通了,请讲。

11. Would you like to try the extension?
    您要不要试试分机?

12. For inside call, you can dial the room number directly.
    打内部电话,您直接拨打房号就可以了。

13. For local call, dial 9 first, then the number you want.
    打本地电话,先拨 9,再拨您要拨打的电话号码。

14. For DDD call, dial 9 first, then the area code, and the number you want at last.
    国内长途直拨,先拨 9,再拨区号,最后拨当地电话号码。

15. Local calls from hotel rooms are free of charge.
    在酒店房间内拨打市内电话是免费的。

Section B

Service Procedure 服务流程

1. Greet the guest with Good Morning / Afternoon, and identify your department or your hotel.
   问候客人(早上好/下午好)并自报你所在的部门或酒店。

2. Ask whether the guest needs your help.

询问客人是否需要帮助。

3. Offer assistance and take notes.

   提供帮助并做好记录。

4. Always confirm every detail of information you are given.

   要确认你所获得的所有细节。

5. When transferring a call, inform the guest that you are going to do this.

   当你要转接电话时,应告知客人你要这么做。

6. Bid farewell to the guest.

   与客人道别。

7. Wait for the caller to hang up first.

   等来电者先挂机。

Ⅰ. Service Performance 服务演练

G＝Guest（客人）　　　　O＝Operator（话务员）

O：Good evening, Holiday Inn. What can I do for you?

　　晚上好,假日酒店。能够为您做些什么?

G：Good evening. I'd like to know how to make a call.

　　晚上好。我想知道如何拨打电话。

O：For room to room calls, dial room number directly please. For local calls, first dial 9, then the number you want.

　　如果您拨打房间对房间的电话,直接拨房号就可以了;如果您拨打本地电话,先拨9,再拨您要拨打的电话。

G：Thank you. I'd like to make an international call to New York. What should I do then?

　　谢谢。我想打国际长途电话到纽约,我该怎么办?

O：You may call directly from your room. Dial 9 first, then the country code, then area code and at last the number you want.

　　先生,您可以直接从房间拨打。先拨9,再拨国家代码和区号,最后拨打当地号码。

G：I see. Thanks a lot. By the way, what time is it in New York now?

　　我明白了,多谢。顺便问一声,纽约现在几点?

O：There is a time difference of 13 hours. It's 9 o'clock in the morning.

　　时差是13个小时。纽约现在是上午9点。

G：I'd like to make a call now. You are so helpful.

　　我现在就想打一个电话,你给了我很大的帮助。

O: You're welcome, sir. I'm always at your service.
不客气，先生，我很乐意为您效劳。

Ⅱ. Position Practice 岗位实训

★ Transfer a call. （转接电话）

1. I'd like to transfer your call to the Front Office.
   我把您的电话转到前台。
2. I'm sorry the line is busy. Would you care to please hold on for a moment?
   很抱歉电话占线，您介意稍等一会儿吗？
3. The line isn't busy now. I'll put you through.
   电话不占线了，我给您接过去。
4. Well, the phone is through, go ahead, please.
   好了，电话通了，请讲话。

★ Confirm payment methods. （确认付款方式）

1. Could I know how you will be paying for this call? Is it a collect call or a paid call?
   请问您用何种方式付这个电话费？是对方付费还是您自己付费？
2. This is the hotel operator. I have a collect call from Mr. Smith in London. Will you accept the charges?
   这里是酒店总机，史密斯先生从伦敦打来电话，是由接听人付费的，您愿意付款吗？

★ Take a message. （记录口信）

1. I'm afraid there's no reply from room 1618.
   恐怕1618房没有人接听。
2. Would you like to leave a message?
   您要留言吗？
3. I'll put you through to the message desk.
   我帮您接通留言台。

★ Wake-up call. （叫醒服务）

1. What time would you like your morning call?
   您要几点叫早？
2. May I have your name and room number please?
   请告诉我您的名字和房号好吗？

Ⅲ. Listening Practice 听力实训

★ A. Listen to the conversation and take the caller's message.

Blue Beach Hotel

To: _____

From: _____

Message: _____

★ B. Complete the following dialogue.

Operator: White Swan Hotel. Can I help you?

Caller: Yes, my flight is 6:00 o'clock tomorrow morning. _____.

Operator: Sure, _____?

Caller: How long will it take to go to the airport?

Operator: About 30 minutes.

Caller: Then 4:30 a.m. will be OK.

Operator: Yes, and _____?

Caller: Certainly. Mr. Spink, room 1215.

Operator: Thank you sir, _____.

Caller: Thank you very much, have a good night.

Operator: Have a good night.

Important 特别关注

▲ Make sure to be prepared for all calls and have a positive attitude.
确保用积极的态度接听所有来电。

▲ Pick up the phone within three rings.
电话铃响三声之内接电话。

▲ Protect guest's private information.
保护客人的个人信息。

▲ Don't slam the receiver.
放置话筒时要轻。

▲ Use no jargon.
不使用行话、黑话。

▲ Be friendly, don't end a call hurriedly.
结束电话时态度要友好，不能仓促。

▲ Wait for the caller to hang up first.
等来电者先挂机。

Section C

Case and Development 案例与创新

Case 案例

Guest: You are a new check-in guest at this hotel, and you want to make a collect call to Paris. But you don't know how to do it. You are calling the operator to ask for help.

Operator: You answer the phone and tell the guest how to make an international call from his room. You also tell the guest that the hotel will collect 8 yuan for a collect call.

Development 创新

• What information will an operator learn if someone calls and asks him to leave a message to a registered guest in the hotel?

• Should the operator check with the caller after he hears all the information?

• What kind of rules shall you bear in mind when doing your job as an operator?

技能实训 8 外币兑换服务
Foreign Currency Exchange

Section A

Basic Knowledge for Position 岗位基础知识

I. Word Stock 词库

cashier	收银员
exchange	兑换
one-way exchange	单向兑换
full exchange	全向兑换
today's exchange rate	今天的汇率
exchange memo	兑换水单
currency	货币
foreign currency	外币
foreign exchange counter	外币柜台
receipt	收据
double check	双核对
Bank of China	中国银行

II. Pronunciation 语音训练

1. I'd like to exchange some Euros into RMB.
   我想把一些欧元换成人民币。
2. Where can I exchange foreign currency?
   我在哪里可以兑换外币?
3. What's today's exchange rate?
   今天的汇率是多少?
4. How much would you like to exchange?
   您要兑换多少?
5. Do you accept traveler's check?
   你这里接受旅行支票吗?
6. I'd like to cash this traveler's check.

请将这些旅行支票换成现金。

7. I'd like some small change.
   请帮忙换一些零钱。

8. May I see your passport, please?
   能看一下您的护照吗?

9. Would you please fill in this exchange memo?
   请您填一下这张兑换水单好吗?

10. The exchange rate of US dollar to RMB is 1∶7.2.
    美元兑人民币的汇率是1∶7.2。

11. The total is 3960 RMB, please have a check.
    总共是3960元人民币,请核对。

12. Please keep the exchange memo well and you may need it.
    保管好兑换水单,也许您会用得上。

13. You can go to the Bank of China or the airport exchange office if you want to change it back into US dollars by showing the exchang memo.
    如果您要把它换回美元,出示您的兑换水单,您可以去中国银行或机场的外币兑换处。

Section B

Service Procedure 服务流程

1. Greetings.
   问候。

2. Ask what kind of foreign currency the guest would like to exchange.
   询问需要兑换的外币种类。

3. Introduce today's exchange rate.
   介绍当天的汇率。

4. Confirm how much the guest would like to exchange.
   确认客人需要兑换的数额。

5. Check guest's passport.
   查看客人的护照。

6. Fill in the exchange memo.
   填写外汇兑换水单。

7. Tell the guest the amount he could have.
   告诉客人能兑换的金额。

8. Give the money and ask the guest to have a check.

   把兑换的钱给客人并请他核对。

9. Give the receipt and ask him to keep it well.

   给客人收据并请他妥善保管。

Ⅰ. Service Performance 服务演练

G＝Guest（客人）　　　C＝Cashier of foreign exchange counter（外币兑换柜台收银员）

C：Good afternoon, sir. Is there anything I can do for you?

　　先生，下午好。有什么可以为您效劳的吗？

G：I'd like to exchange some US dollars into Chinese RMB.

　　我想把一些美元换成人民币。

C：According to today's exchange rate, every 100 US dollars comes to 720 RMB. How much would you like to exchange, sir?

　　根据今天的汇率，每100美元换720元人民币。先生，您要换多少？

G：Well, I'll exchange 300 dollars. Here you are.

　　我想换300美元。给你。

C：Would you please fill in this exchange memo and show me your passport?

　　您能不能填一下兑换水单并出示您的护照？

G：Here you are. Is that all right?

　　给你！你看行吗？

C：That's all right. Thanks. What would you want for your money?

　　行，谢谢！您要什么面值的货币？

G：Any kind will be OK. But I'd like some ten-yuan and fifty-yuan notes.

　　都行，最好有一些10元、50元的零钞。

C：Here is 2160 Yuan. Please have a check. And here's your exchange memo. Please keep it well. You can go to the Bank of China or the airport exchange if you want to change it back into dollars by showing the exchange memo.

　　这是2160元，请核对一下。这是您的兑换水单，请妥善保管。如果您要把它换回美元，您可以去中国银行或机场的外币兑换处，出示您的兑换水单。

G：Thank you very much.

　　非常感谢！

C：My pleasure.

　　乐意为您效劳。

Ⅱ. Position Practice 岗位实训

★ English names and symbols of some common currencies.（常见的货币符号及英文名称）

1. CNY（Chinese Yuan）人民币

2. HKD（Hong Kong Dollar）港元
3. USD（United States Dollar）美元
4. EUR（European Dollar）欧元
5. CAD（Canadian Dollar）加拿大元
6. NZD（New Zealand Dollar）新西兰元
7. SGD（Singapore Dollar）新加坡元
8. AUD（Australian Dollar）澳大利亚元
9. GBP（Great Britain Pound）英镑
10. JPY（Japanese Yen）日元
11. KRW（South Korean Won）韩币
12. THB（Thai Baht）泰铢
13. CHF（Swiss Franc）瑞士法郎
14. MYR（Malaysian Ringgit）马来西亚令吉

★ Some common types of international credit cards.（几种国际通用的信用卡）
1. Visa Card 维萨卡
2. Mastercard 万事达卡
3. Eurocard（EC）欧洲卡
4. American Express Credit Card 美国运通卡
5. International Diner's Club Card 国际大来俱乐部卡
6. JCB Credit Card　JCB 信用卡
7. Federal Bank Credit Card 联邦银行信用卡
8. Great Wall Card 长城卡

Ⅲ．Listening Practice 听力实训

★ A. Fill the information in the following exchange memo.

Valentine's Island Resort

Purchased from ＿＿＿＿＿＿＿＿　　Date ＿＿＿＿＿＿＿＿
Room ＿＿＿＿＿＿＿＿　　　　　　Passport No. ＿＿＿＿＿＿＿＿
Currency Amount ＿＿＿＿＿＿＿＿　Exchange Rate ＿＿＿＿＿＿＿＿
RMB Equivalent ＿＿＿＿＿＿＿＿
Guest Signature ＿＿＿＿＿＿＿＿
Authorized Signature & Stamp ＿＿＿＿＿＿＿＿

★ B. Complete the following dialogue.
Guest：I'd like to exchange some Euros，please.
Cashier：＿＿＿＿＿＿＿＿＿＿＿＿＿＿＿＿＿＿＿＿＿＿＿＿＿＿＿＿＿＿＿＿？

Guest: Yes. Here's my room card.
Cashier: _____?
Guest: 500 Euros, please. _____?
Cashier: It's 7.3 yuan to one Euro... So that's a _____.
Guest: Thank you.
Cashier: _____.

Important 特别关注

▲ Since currency exchange rates vary from place to place and day to day, where and how you exchange currency can make a difference.
因为每个地区每一天的汇率可能都不一样,所以你在不同的地方、采取不同的方式兑换外币会产生一些差异。

▲ Do keep in mind that credit card companies may ask an additional fee for overseas usage. If you're not sure, check with your bank before you leave home.
记住:有些信用卡公司对在海外使用的信用卡要收取额外的费用。如果你不确定,在出国之前与发卡银行核对一下。

▲ Some countries' currency and exchange rate are more changeable than others because of their inflation and unstable economies.
因为通货膨胀和经济不稳定的原因,有些国家的货币或汇率比其他国家要更加多变。

Section C

Case and Development 案例与创新

Case 案例

Guest: You want to exchange some Euros into RMB. You go through the necessary formalities on request. You find there is something wrong with the amount of the RMB the cashier gives you.

Cashier: You make clear what kind of currency the guest has got and tell him the exchange rate. You accept the foreign currency and ask the guest to go through the formalities. You correct the mistake and apologize.

Development 创新

- Why don't most hotels accept personal checks?
- Why is it much safer to buy traveler's checks than carry a lot of cash?
- What are advantages and disadvantages of using credit cards in our daily life?

技能实训 9 结账退房服务 Check Out

Section A

Basic Knowledge for Position 岗位基础知识

听力音频

Ⅰ. Word Stock 词库

cashier	收银员
cash	现金
credit card	信用卡
traveler's check	旅行支票
change	零钱
exchange receipt	兑换收据
personal check	私人支票
pay in cash	用现金付款
pay by credit card	用信用卡付款
pay with a traveler's check	用旅行支票付款
sign the bill	签单
transfer	转账
invoice	发票
refund	退款
Dragon Card	龙卡
Peony Card	牡丹卡

Ⅱ. Pronunciation 语音训练

1. May I have your room card, please?
   请把房卡交给我好吗?
2. Just a moment, please. The cashier will have your bill ready in a moment.
   请稍等,收银员马上会准备好您的账单。
3. Thank you for waiting, sir. Here is your bill. Would you like to check it?
   先生,让您久等了。这是您的账单,要核对一下吗?

4. Excuse me, sir, did you use the mini bar this morning?
   先生，请问上午您消费过小冰箱里的东西吗？

5. 2000 yuan in total.
   总共 2000 元。

6. How would you like to pay, madam?
   女士，您用哪种方式付款？

7. What kind of credit card have you got?
   您持有哪种信用卡？

8. I'm sorry, we don't accept personal checks according to the hotel rules.
   对不起，根据酒店的规定，我们不收个人支票。

9. Would you like to settle the difference in cash?
   您愿意用现金支付差额吗？

10. I'm terribly sorry for the inconvenience.
    给您带来不便真的十分抱歉。

11. I neglected that detail when I drew your bill.
    我在开账单时忽略了那个细节。

12. I'll correct your bill, would you mind waiting for a minute?
    我将把账单改正过来，您介意稍等片刻吗？

13. Here is the money you overpaid.
    这是您多付的钱。

14. May I have your signature, please?
    请您签个名好吗？

15. Here is your card and receipt.
    这是您的卡和收据。

16. I'll call the bellman to take your baggage down.
    我会叫服务员把您的行李拿下来。

Section B

Service Procedure 服务流程

1. Greetings.
   问候。

2. Confirm the departure.
   确认离店。

3. Ask the guest's name and the room number.
   询问客人的名字和房号。

4. Ask the guest to return the room card.
   要求客人交回房卡。

5. Confirm the method of the payment.
   确认客人的付款方式。

6. Tell the guest to have a check about the bill.
   要求客人核查账单总数。

7. Bid farewell to the guest.
   与客人道别。

Ⅰ. **Service Performance 服务演练**

G＝Guest（客人）　　　C＝Cashier（收银员）

C：Good morning, madam. May I help you?
   上午好，女士。有什么可以帮您的吗？

G：Yes, I want to check out now.
   是的，我要结账。

C：May I have your room number and room card, please?
   告诉我您的房号并交回房卡，好吗？

G：Room 1234, and here is the room card.
   1234 房间，这是房卡。

C：Did you use mini bar this morning?
   今天上午您使用过小冰箱吗？

C：Yes, I had some drinks.
   是的，我喝过饮料。

G：Just a moment please, the cashier will have your bill ready in a moment.
   请稍等，收银员一会儿就会把您的账算好。
   (After a while.)（过了一会儿。）

C：I am sorry to keep you waiting. The total bill is 1200 yuan, madam.
   很抱歉让您久等了。女士，总数是 1200 元。

G：Would you mind letting me check the bill?
   您在意我核对一下账单吗？

C：Not at all, please.
   当然不，请吧。

G：I'm sorry, I think you made some mistakes. I don't think I consumed that much. I did not understand what that charge is for.
   不好意思，我认为您弄错了。我认为我没有消费那么多，我不明白那个项目是干什么的。

C：Let me see… That is the charge of your calls, madam.
让我看一下……女士，那是您打电话的费用。

G：Yes, I remember now. That's OK. Do you accept credit cards?
哦，我想起来了，这就对了。你们接受信用卡付款吗？

C：Yes. We certainly accept credit card and what kind of card have you got?
是的，我们接受信用卡。您手中持有哪种信用卡？

G：I have Mastercard, here you are.
我持有万事达卡，给你。

C：Thank you. Would you please sign your name here?
谢谢。请在这儿签名好吗？

G：Certainly.
好的。

C：Thank you, madam. Here is your receipt. We are looking forward to seeing you again, goodbye.
谢谢您，女士。这是您的收据。我们期待再次为您提供服务，再见。

Ⅱ. Position Practice 岗位实训

★ The guest pays in cash. （客人用现金付款）
Here is your change and receipt. Please have a check.
这是找您的钱和收据，请核对。

★ The guest pay by credit card. （客人用信用卡付款）
1. May I take a print of your card?
   我能够刷一下您的卡吗？
2. Would you please sign your name here?
   请您在这里签名好吗？
3. I'm afraid it is not enough to cover the amount.
   恐怕卡里的金额不够。

★ Exchange foreign currency. （兑换外币）
1. The exchange rate of US dollar to RMB is 1∶7.2, that will be RMB 2010.
   今天的汇率是1美元兑7.2元人民币，这样可以兑换人民币2010元。
2. I'm afraid that we only offer one-way exchange.
   恐怕我们只能提供单方的兑换。
3. Would you like it in small changes or big bills?
   您是要零钞还是大钞？

★ Deal with miscalculation. （处理误算）
1. There is a mistake.
   这里有错误。

2. I'll check it with relevant departments.
   我会跟有关部门核对。

3. I'm awfully sorry for the mistake. I assure you it won't happen again.
   出现这种错误我真的十分抱歉。我向您保证这样的错误不会再发生。

4. I do apologize for the mistake.
   我为发生这样的错误真诚地向您道歉。

★ Bid farewell to the guest.（向客人道别）

1. I hope you enjoyed your stay with us.
   我希望您过得愉快！

2. We look forward to serving you again.
   我期待再次为您服务。

Ⅲ. Listening Practice 听力实训

★ A. Listen to the conversation and fill in the hotel bill with the information you hear.

Name：		No. of Persons：	
Nationality：		Date：	
Room Number：		Rate：	
1	Room Number		
2	Meals		
3		72.00	
4	City Tour		
5	Bar		
6		60.00	
7	Room Service		
8		1950.00	
9	Total		

★ B. Complete the following dialogue.

Cashier：Good morning, madam. How may I help you?

Guest：I'd like to check out now.

Cashier：_____?

Guest：Klinda Fox in Room 2306, _____.

Cashier：_____?

Guest：Yes, I had a bottle of beer.

Cashier：One moment please. Let me prepare the bill for you.

...
Cashier: _____. Your bill is total 2800 yuan, _____. Please have a check.

Guest: That's OK.

Cashier: You have paid 1000 yuan deposit, haven't you?

Guest: Yes, here's the deposit receipt.

Cashier: Then _____?

Guest: In cash, here is the money.

Cashier: Thank you, here is the receipt. _____.

Guest: Thank you, goodbye.

Cashier: Goodbye, have a nice day.

Important 特别关注

▲ Check if the guest's credit card is in the black list. If it's in the black list or the amount is not enough to cover the expenses, inform the guest to make the payment in another way.

应检查客人的信用卡是否在黑名单中。若发现客人的信用卡在黑名单上或者客人的信用卡账户余额不足,应及时通知客人改用其他方式付款。

▲ The guests are required to produce the traveler's check with his own signature and his own valid identification certificate, and countersign it on the counter. If both signatures are in conformity, cash can be withdrawn at once.

客人需出具本人签发的旅行支票和本人有效身份证件并在收银柜台当场复签,双签核对相符后即可办理兑付现金。

Section C

Case and Development 案例与创新

Case 案例

Guest: You want to check out. You notice a mistake on the bill. You are a nonsmoker, but you are charged for a pack of cigarettes. You want to know if they'll take a traveler's check. And that's all you have got.

Cashier: The guest wants the bill, so you tell him you'll be along in a moment. Apologize for the mistake.

Development 创新

- Do you know how many ways in which the guests can usually pay their hotel bills?
- What can you do when you notice the guest is in the black list?
- Why can a cashier's work be dangerous sometimes?

技能实训 10　商务中心服务 Business Center

Section A

Basic Knowledge for Position 岗位基础知识

I. Word Stock 词库

typing (n.) /type (v.)	打字
copying (n.) /copy (v.)	复印
copier	复印机
document	文件
original	原件
fax	传真
express	快件
EMS (Express Mail Service)	特快专递
registered letter	挂号信
enlarge	放大
reduce	缩小
folder	文件夹
airmail	航空邮件
addressee	收信人
surface mail	平邮
postage	邮费
zip code/postal code	邮编

II. Pronunciation 语音训练

1. I'd like to copy my ID card/my passport.
   我想复印我的身份证/我的护照。
2. I'd like to send a parcel. How much is the postage?
   我要寄一个包裹，邮费是多少钱？
3. How many copies would you like?
   您要复印多少份？

4. Would you like me to make the color a little darker or a little lighter?
   您要我把颜色调深一点还是淡一点？
5. Shall I copy these on both sides of the paper?
   我进行双面复印好吗？
6. Your original is not very clear. I can't guarantee the copy will be good.
   您的原件不太清晰，我不能保证复印件的效果很好。
7. I'm sorry. The machine is out of order.
   很抱歉，机器出了故障。
8. I'll call you as soon as the machine is fixed.
   机器一修好我就给您打电话。
9. Sending a fax to New York is 10 yuan per minute, including service charge.
   发传真到纽约每分钟10元，包括服务费。
10. Mr. Brown, this is Business Center. We have received a fax for you.
    布朗先生，这里是商务中心。我们收到给您的一份传真。

Section B

Service Procedure 服务流程

1. Greetings.
   问候。
2. Ask for the requirements of the guest.
   询问客人的需求。
3. Confirm the requirements and meet the guest's demand fully.
   确认并充分满足客人的需求。
4. Explain the service charge and make sure of the method of payment.
   说明资费标准并弄清付款方式。
5. Confirm the guest's name and the room number.
   确认客人的姓名和房号。
6. Bid farewell to the guest.
   与客人道别。

I. Service Performance 服务演练

G= Guest（客人）　　　C=Clerk of Business Center（商务中心职员）

C：Good afternoon, madam. What can I do for you?
　　下午好，女士。有什么能为您效劳的吗？

G：Yes. I'd like to have these copied.
　　我想复印这些资料。

C：Certainly. How many copies would you like?
　　好的。您想复印多少份？

G：Three copies for each.
　　每张三份。

C：That's all right.
　　行。
　　（After a while.）（过了一会儿。）

C：Here you are.
　　给您。

G：Thanks. And can you send a fax for me?
　　谢谢。你能帮我发一份传真吗？

C：To where?
　　发往哪里？

G：To Chicago. What's the rate?
　　发往芝加哥。你们如何收费？

C：To Chicago it's 10 yuan per minute, excluding service charge.
　　发往芝加哥每分钟10元，不包括服务费。

G：OK. Please send it right now. It's urgent.
　　好的，现在就发吧，这是急件。

C：No problem, madam.
　　没问题，女士。

G：Thank you.
　　谢谢。

C：How would you like to make payment, madam?
　　女士，您想如何付款？

G：Go with my room charge.
　　记入房费吧。

C：Would you please show me your room card?
　　请出示您的房卡好吗？

G：Here you are.
　　给你。

C: Thank you. Could you please sign here?
   谢谢。请您在这儿签字好吗？

G: Sure.
   好的。

Ⅱ. Position Practice 岗位实训

★ Type documents for guests. （为客人打印文档）

1. What font and size would you like?
   您要什么字体、几号字？

2. Shall I make the space larger?
   我把行距拉开一些好吗？

3. I'm afraid we only save it on our disks, in case of any virus.
   恐怕我只能把它存在我们的磁盘上，以防有病毒。

★ Send a fax for guests. （为客人发传真）

1. The minimum charge is 20 yuan, including service charge.
   最低收费是 20 元，包括服务费。

2. Please write down the country code, the area code and his number.
   请写下国家代码、区号和对方的号码。

3. Shall I make a copy of this, and then send the copy?
   我复印一份，然后将复印件传真过去好吗？

★ Explain machine is out of order to guests. （向客人解释故障）

1. The paper is jammed.
   卡纸了。

2. It is out of ink.
   没墨了。

3. The machine is out of order.
   机器出故障了。

4. A repairman is coming to fix it soon.
   修理工很快就过来。

★ Tickets Service. （票务服务）

1. Which day's ticket would you like?
   您要哪天的票？

2. First class or economy class?
   头等舱还是经济舱？

3. One way or a round trip ticket?
   单程票还是双程票？

4. I'm afraid that the flight is fully booked.
   恐怕那个航班的票已经订完了。

Ⅲ． Listening Practice 听力实训

★ A. Listen to the conversation and fill the information in the fax sending and receiving form.

Guest Name		Room No.	
Fax No. _____ Charge _____ Signature _____			To Country _____ Payment by _____
Remarks			

★ B. Complete the following dialogue.

Clerk： Good morning, sir. _____?

Guest： Yes. I'd like you to _____ for me.

Clerk： What is it?

Guest： It's a company document.

Clerk： _____?

Guest： What do you offer?

Clerk： There are two ways, _____.

Guest： Overnight delivery. What's the charge?

Clerk： It's 20 yuan for your express mail. _____.

Guest： Here you are.

Clerk： And your telephone number?

Guest： 1368871××××.

Clerk： _____?

Guest： Go with room charge please.

Clerk： That's fine. Goodbye.

Guest： Goodbye.

Important 特别关注

▲ Don't conduct any banking or confidential business via the PC of the Business Center.
不要在商务中心的电脑上进行金融或保密交易。

▲ When you return to your home or office, change any passwords of the accounts you have accessed through the PC of the Business Center.
当你回到家或办公室，应该马上改变在商务中心用过的个人电脑上的账户密码。

▲ Keep secret. Do not tell the content of fax to any person who has nothing to do with it.

做好保密工作。不得随意向他人谈及客人的传真件内容。

Section C

Case and Development 案例与创新

Case 案例

Mr. Johnson, a hotel guest in room 1716, comes to the Business Center at 10 a.m. He asks Miss Lin to type some documents for him. Miss Lin tells him the charge will be 7 yuan per page excluding service charge. The guest wants Miss Lin to have the work done and send the documents to his room before 4 p.m.

Development 创新

• What shall you do if the guest tells you he has no time to check what you have typed?

• What shall you do when there is a fax for a guest who has checked out?

• What are the key points of fax services in the Business Center?

实训模块三

客房服务
Housekeeping

Housekeeping is perhaps the most important support department in Front Office. It is responsible for cleaning the guest rooms and making them look tidy and comfortable. To ensure speedy, efficient rooming of guests in vacant and ready rooms, the Housekeeping and Front Office must inform each other promptly of any changes in a room's status or availability. Only by doing this can the guests feel the warmth and live comfortably in "home away from home."

客房部是前厅部最主要的辅助部门,主要负责客房的清洁卫生,使客房看起来整洁、舒适。为保证空房被高效有序地分配,前厅部和客房部对客房的状态和入住率要及时互通信息。只有这样,客人才能体会到"家外之家"的温馨与舒适。

技能实训 11 打扫房间 Room Cleaning

Section A
Basic Knowledge for Position 岗位基础知识

I. Word Stock 词库

room attendant	客房服务员
housekeeper	客房部经理
towel	毛巾
bathing towel	浴巾
tissue	面巾纸
toilet paper	卫生纸
soap	香皂
shampoo	洗发水
shower cap	浴帽
shower	淋浴
bathrobe	浴袍
toothbrush	牙刷
toothpaste	牙膏
hanger	衣架
sheet	床单
pillow	枕头
blanket	毯子
slipper	拖鞋
ashtray	烟灰缸
bed cover	床罩
quilt	被子
shaver	剃须刀
curtain	窗帘
electric kettle	电开水壶
trash bin	垃圾桶

Ⅱ. Pronunciation 语音训练

1. Housekeeping. May I come in?
   客房服务,可以进来吗?

2. I'm your room attendant, I'm sorry to bother you, may I clean your room now?
   我是客房服务员,很抱歉打扰您,现在可以清理您的房间吗?

3. What time will be convenient for you, sir?
   先生,您什么时候方便?

4. Is there anything else I can do for you?
   还有其他可以为您做的吗?

5. I'm always at your service.
   我很乐意为您效劳。

6. Just a moment please. I'll bring it to your room immediately.
   稍等片刻,我马上拿到您的房间。

7. I will send a repairman to your room at once.
   我马上派一位维修人员到您的房间来。

Section B

Service Procedure 服务流程

1. Knock at the door gently three times.
   轻轻地敲门三次。

2. Say: "Housekeeping. May I come in?"
   问:"客房服务,可以进来吗?"

3. Greet the guest when allowed to enter the room.
   当得到客人的许可进入房间时,向客人问候。

4. Ask the guest whether it is convenient to clean the room now.
   询问客人现在能否打扫房间。

5. Clean the room.
   打扫房间。
   Open the window.
   开窗。
   Empty the trash bin.
   倒垃圾。

Make the bed.

整理床。

Clean the bathroom.

清洁卫生间。

Replenish the supplies.

补充客房物品。

Vacuum the floor.

吸尘。

Self-check.

自查。

6. Express your good wishes.

表达祝愿。

I. Service Performance 服务演练

G＝ Guest（客人）　　　R＝Room Attendant（客房服务员）

R：(Knocking at the door three times) Housekeeping. May I come in?

（轻轻地敲三下门）客房服务，可以进来吗？

G：Come in please.

请进。

R：Good morning, sir. May I clean your room now?

早上好，先生。我现在可以清理您的房间吗？

G：You'd better not. You see, we are having some friends over. We're going to have an appointment in the room.

您最好不要清理。有几个朋友马上要过来，我们将在这儿见面。

R：Certainly, sir. What time will be convenient for you?

好的，先生。那您什么时候方便？

G：Would you please come back in two hours?

你能两个小时以后再过来吗？

R：No problem. I'll clean up your room in two hours.

没问题。我两个小时以后过来清理您的房间。

G：That's fine… Well, our friends seem to be a little late. Would you please tidy up the bathroom? I've just taken a bath.

好的……我的朋友看来要晚点到，你能否清理一下卫生间？我刚刚洗过澡。

R：Sure, sir.

好的，先生。

(Finishing cleaning the bathroom.) （清理好卫生间之后）

R：Is there anything else I can do for you, sir?

先生，还有什么可以为您做的吗？

G：Oh, yes. Where can I get another pair of slippers?

哦，我在哪儿可以再拿一双拖鞋？

R：I'll send one up right away.

我马上给您拿一双过来。

G：Thank you. You are always friendly and helpful.

谢谢，你总是这么友好和乐于助人。

R：You're welcome. I'm always at your service.

不客气，很乐意为您效劳。

Ⅱ. Position Practice 岗位实训

★ Room Status. （客房状态）

1. VC（Vacant Clean）已清扫空房

2. VD（Vacant Dirty）未清扫空房

3. OD（Occupied Dirty）未清扫住客房

4. OC（Occupied Clean）已清扫住客房

5. OOO（Out Of Order）待修房，维修房

6. ECO（Estimated Check Out）预计退房

7. NS（No Smoking）无烟房

8. S/O（Slept Out）外睡房

9. D/L（Double Lock）双锁房

10. DND（Do Not Disturb）请勿打扰

11. MUR（Make Up Room）请即打扫房

12. RS（Refuse Service）拒绝服务

13. N/B（No Baggage）无行李

14. L/B（Light Baggage）少行李

15. VIP（Very Important People）重要客人

16. LSG（Long Staying Guest）长住客

17. C/O（Check Out）结账

18. C/I（Check In）入住

★ What kind of rooms will be cleaned first?（先清扫哪一类房间？）

1. If the room occupancy is high, the room attendant will clean the rooms in the following order: Make Up Room, VIP, Vacant Dirty, Occupied Dirty, Long Staying Guest and Vacant Clean.

入住率高时，客房打扫按下列顺序：请即打扫房、VIP 房、未清扫空房、未清扫住客房、长住房、已清扫空房。

2. If the room occupancy is low, the room attendant will clean the rooms in the following order: Make Up Room, VIP, Occupied Dirty, Long Staying Guest, Vacant Dirty and Vacant Clean.

入住率低时，客房打扫按下列顺序：请即打扫房、VIP 房、未清扫空房、长住房、退房、已清扫空房。

★ Knocking at the door.（敲门）

1. First check if there is "DND" sign on the door or if it is a double lock room.

首先检查一下房门是否挂着"请勿打扰"牌或上"双锁"。

2. Knock at the door three times gently and say: " Housekeeping."

轻轻敲三下门，同时报身份："客房服务。"

3. Wait 10 seconds to see the reactions inside. If there is no answer, please knock at the door once again.

在门外等候 10 秒钟，倾听房内动静，若无反应，可再次尝试敲门。

★ Opening the door.（开门）

1. After confirming there is no one in the room, open the door slightly and say: "May I come in?" Only after that you can enter the room.

在确认房内无动静后，轻轻将门打开，报明自己的身份，询问"可以进来吗"后，方可进入。

2. If the guest is in the room, you can only enter the room with guest's permission, you should greet the guest and ask if you can clean the room.

如果客人在房内，要经客人同意后方可进入，并向客人问候，询问客人"是否可以打扫房间"。

★ Checking the mini bar.（检查小冰箱）

If you find the guest has consumed some drinks and wine in the mini bar, you should fill in the wine list and send it to the cashier in the Front Office. You should refill the mini bar as well.

发现已消费的酒水，填写酒水单，在下班时递交前台收银处并将小冰箱重新装满。

Ⅲ. **Listening Practice** 听力实训

★ A. Listen to the recording and complete the conversation.

Room attendant: _____?

Guest: Come in, please.

Room attendant: Good morning, sir. _____?

Guest: Not now, I have a bad headache.

Room attendant: _____. Shall I get you a doctor?

Guest: Not necessary. Could you give me some aspirin tablets?

Room attendant: Oh, I'm sorry, _____.

Guest: I see. I just need a good rest.

Room attendant: Let me put out _____. If you remove it, I'll know you want me to clean your room.

Guest: All right.

Room attendant: _____.

★ B. Listen to the recording and tell what a room attendant should do and should not do while making up the guest room. Write "√" for what a room attendant should do, write "×" for what a room attendant should not do.

1. vacuuming the carpet (   )
2. changing linens (   )
3. offering laundry service (   )
4. replacing the toilet needs and toilet facilities (   )
5. refilling the mini bar (   )
6. making extra bed for the guest (   )
7. looking after the guest's child on request (   )
8. buying medicine for the guest if he doesn't feel well (   )

Important 特别关注

▲ The room attendant can tidy up the guest's documents, magazines and newspapers a bit but he should always put them in the right order and never read them.
清扫时将客人的文件、杂志、书报稍加整理，但不能弄错位置，更不能翻看。

▲ Never throw away the guest's empty bottles or paper boxes of cosmetic even if it is used up.
客人自带的化妆品即使使用完了，也不得将空瓶或纸盒扔掉。

▲ Never touch the guest's camera, laptop computer, notebook or wallet.
特别留意不要随意触摸客人的照相机、手提式电脑、笔记本、钱包等物品。

Section C

Case and Development 案例与创新

Case 案例

New Room attendant: You have finished cleaning the room when the guest is out.

You have put the letters, documents and books in good order.

You have picked up a pair of sunglasses out of the trash bin and put it on the writing desk.

The phone on the nightstand keeps ringing again and again. You are worried there might be something urgent for the guest. You'd like to answer the phone for the guest.

Housekeeper: You come to check the room. You tell the new room attendant that the things on the desk concern the guest's privacy.

What is in the trash bin is waste forever.

You stop the new room attendant from answering the phone and tell him the reason.

Development 创新

• What are the differences between the responsibilities of the room attendant and the PA cleaner?

• Would you buy some medicine for the guest when he tells you he doesn't feel well, why or why not?

• What shall you do if you find a guest gets drunk and needs some help?

技能实训 12　洗衣服务 Laundry Service

听力音频

Section A

Basic Knowledge for Position 岗位基础知识

I. Word Stock 词库

laundry	洗衣房；要（或正在）洗的衣物；刚洗好的衣物
laundry form	洗衣单
laundry bag	洗衣袋
collect your laundry	收取衣服
express service	快洗服务
dry cleaning	干洗
machine wash	机洗
hand washing	手洗
rinsing	水洗
do not wash	不能水洗
ironing	熨烫
valet	洗衣工
shrink	缩水
blouse	女衬衣
bow-tie	领结
evening dress	晚礼服
jacket	夹克衫
skirt	裙子
scarf	围巾
pullover	套头毛衣，套衫
sweater	毛衣
jeans	牛仔裤
T-shirt	T恤衫
socks	短袜
trousers	裤子

suit	西装
overcoat	外套，大衣
cheongsam	旗袍
pajamas	睡衣
stockings	长袜

Ⅱ. Pronunciation 语音训练

1. I have some laundry to be done.
   我有些衣服要洗。

2. My dress needs dry cleaning.
   我的衣服需要干洗。

3. My trousers need to be mended.
   我的裤子需要缝补。

4. Do you have any laundry? / Have you got any laundry?
   您有要洗的衣服吗？

5. May I know your name and room number?
   可以告诉我您的名字和房号吗？

6. A valet will be up in a few minutes.
   洗衣工几分钟之后就到。

7. Laundry service. May I come in?
   洗衣服务，可以进来吗？

8. I'm here to collect your laundry.
   我过来取您的衣服。

9. You can find the laundry form in the drawer of the writing desk.
   您可以在写字桌的抽屉里找到洗衣单。

10. You can leave the laundry bag in the bathroom.
    您可以把洗衣袋放在卫生间里。

11. Could you please fill in the laundry form?
    请您填写一下洗衣单好吗？

12. How would you like your laundry to be done? Dry cleaning, hand washing or just ironing?
    您的衣服要怎么洗？干洗，手洗，还是只熨烫一下？

13. The laundry will be sent back to your room by 6 p.m.
    您的衣服在下午6点之前送回来。

14. We offer express service, but you have to pay 50% extra.
    我们提供快洗服务，但要加收50%的洗衣费。

15. What will be done if there is any laundry damaged?
    如果衣服洗坏了怎么办？
16. Will it shrink? Will the color fade?
    会缩水吗？会褪色吗？
17. I'm sorry to give you so much trouble. May I have your room number please? I'll send your laundry back soon.
    很抱歉给您添了这么多的麻烦。能告诉我您的房号吗？我马上把您的衣服送过去。

Section B

Service Procedure 服务流程

1. Greetings.
   问候。
2. Ask the guest's name and room number.
   询问客人的名字和房号。
3. Collect the laundry and laundry form.
   收取要洗的衣服和洗衣单。
   Ask the guest to fill in the laundry form.
   请客人填写洗衣单。
   Confirm the ways of cleaning.
   确认洗涤方式。
   Any special requirements.
   看看客人是否有特殊要求。
4. Send the laundry back.
   送回洗好的衣服。
5. Ask the guest to check the laundry and sign the name and room number.
   请客人核对并签上名字和房号。
6. Bid farewell to the guest.
   与客人道别。

Ⅰ．Service Performance 服务演练

G＝Guest（客人）　　R＝Room Attendant（客房服务员）

R: Good morning. This is laundry service. What can I do for you?
上午好，这里是洗衣服务，有什么可以帮忙的吗？

G: Could you send someone up for my laundry? Room 908, Mrs. Bell.
能不能派个人过来取衣服？908 房间，贝尔太太。

R: Certainly, Mrs. Bell. A valet will be with you in a few minutes.
当然可以，贝尔太太。洗衣工几分钟后就到您的房间。

G: Good. I also have a silk dress that needs to be washed. Will the color fade in the wash?
好的。我还有一件丝绸的衣服需要清洗。洗的时候衣服会褪色吗？

R: We'll dry clean the dress. Then the color won't fade.
我们将干洗这件衣服，不会褪色的。

G: That's fine. When can I have my laundry back?
那就好。什么时候能送回衣服？

R: Usually it takes about 12 hours to have laundry done. But would you like express service?
一般来说要 12 个小时后。您需要快洗服务吗？

G: What is the difference in price?
价格上有何区别？

R: We charge 50% more for express, but it only takes 4 hours.
快洗服务我们加收 50% 的费用，但只需要 4 个小时。

G: I'll have express then. Where should I leave my laundry?
我选择快洗服务。我把要洗的衣服放在哪儿？

R: Please just leave it in the laundry bag in the bathroom.
请把衣服放在洗衣袋里，然后放在卫生间。

G: I see. Thank you.
我明白了，谢谢。

(In the afternoon)（下午）

R: Laundry service. May I come in?
洗衣服务，可以进来吗？

G: Come in, please.
请进。

R: This is your laundry. Please have a check.
这是您的衣服，请核对一下。

G: How efficient you are!
你们的效率真高！

R: That's all right, madam. Would you please sign your name and room number here?
应该的，女士。在这儿签上您的名字和房号好吗？

G：Sure.
　　好的。

R：Is there anything I can do for you?
　　还有什么要我做的吗?

D：No, thank you. Bye.
　　不用了，谢谢，再见。

R：Bye.
　　再见。

Ⅱ. Position Practice 岗位实训

★ Confirm ways of cleaning.（确认洗涤方式）

1. How would you like your laundry to be cleaned, sir?
   先生，您的衣服要怎么洗?
2. Would you like your silk shirt to be done by hand?
   您的这件丝绸衬衫要手洗吗?
3. Is it to be dry cleaned or for ironing?
   这件是要干洗还是要熨烫一下?

★ Give information about laundry.（提供洗衣信息）

1. It will be ready by 6 o'clock this evening.
   今天晚上 6 点前送达。
2. There is no laundry service on Sundays.
   周日不提供洗衣服务。
3. Laundry collected before 10 a.m. will be returned by 6 p.m. on the same day.
   早上 10 点前收取的衣服将于同一天的下午 6 点前送回。
4. We have a special four-hour express service.
   我们有 4 个小时的快洗服务。
5. We will deliver it within 4 hours at a 50% extra charge.
   4 个小时内送回的衣服我们加收 50%的费用。

★ Apologize when you can't meet the guest's need.（无法满足客人的要求时向客人道歉）

1. I'm afraid we could not remove the stain.
   恐怕我们无法去掉上面的污渍。
2. I'm sorry we can only do simple mending.
   抱歉我们只能做一些简单的修补。
3. I'm terribly sorry we don't have the special equipment to clean leather.
   真的很抱歉我们没有清洗皮料的特制设备。

★ Instructions from the guest. （来自客人的洗衣说明）
1. This sweater will shrink.
   毛衣会缩水。
2. This blouse will fade.
   上衣会褪色。
3. The color will run.
   颜色会扩散。
4. Please use liquid soap.
   请使用液体皂。
5. Please do not use bleach.
   请勿使用漂白剂。
6. Please wash it by water only.
   请用清水漂洗。

★ Laundry Symbols on Clothes Labels. （衣服标签上的洗涤标识）

○ dry-clean 干洗

⊘ do not dry-clean 不可干洗

Ⓟ compatible with any dry cleaning methods 可用各种干洗剂干洗

⊿ iron 熨烫

⊠ do not iron 不可熨烫

△ bleach 可漂白

▲ do not bleach 不可漂白

⊙ tumble dry with no heat 无温转笼干燥

⊗ do not tumble dry 不可转笼干燥

hand wash only 只能手洗

do not wash 不可水洗

Ⅲ. Listening Practice 听力实训

★ A. Listen to the recording and complete the conversation.

Guest：I have some clothes to be washed. Do you have laundry service here?

Room attendant：Yes, sir. _____.

Guest：How long does it usually take to have laundry done?

Room attendant：Usually it takes one day, but _____
_____.

Guest：What's the difference in price?

Room attendant：_____.

Guest: Where can I leave my laundry?

Room attendant: Just _____ . Be sure not to forget to _____ .

Guest: I see. Just one more thing, what if there is any _____ ?

Room attendant: In such a case, the hotel will pay for it, but the indemnity should not _____ .

Guest: That's OK. I hope that won't happen.

Room attendant: Don't worry. The valets are experienced in their work.

★ B. Listen to the recording and tell what a laundry attendant should do and should not do while collecting laundry. Write "√" for what a laundry attendant should do, write "×" for what a laundry attendant should not do.

1. Check if there is any damage on the clothes. (   )
2. Check if there are any items left in the pockets. (   )
3. Confirm the number of clothes. (   )
4. Check the laundry list. (   )
5. Check the washing method carefully, especially special costuming. (   )
6. If there is any missing button, the laundry attendant should mend it for the guest. (   )
7. The laundry attendant will pay for the damage of the laundry. (   )
8. There will be no extra charge for express service in laundry. (   )

Important 特别关注

▲ If DND sign is put on the door of a hotel room, no one shall bother the guest.
  如果门上挂着"请勿打扰"的牌子，请不要打扰客人。

▲ Tell the guest not to forget to fill in the laundry form, otherwise our list must be accepted as correct.
  告诉客人别忘了填写洗衣单，否则以酒店的计数为准。

▲ The hotel is not responsible for valuables in pockets or fastened to garment.
  对于口袋内或系于服装上的贵重物品，酒店概不负责。

Section C

Case and Development 案例与创新

Case 案例

Guest: You have some laundry to be done. Find out if someone can come to your room to collect your laundry. You want to know when you can get it back. You are checking out at 1:00 tomorrow afternoon and need to have it by then.

Housekeeper: The laundry is closed now. There's a laundry bag in the top dresser drawer. If the guest puts his laundry in the bag and leaves it behind the door, the attendant will pick it up early tomorrow morning. He can get the clothes back tomorrow afternoon around 4:00. It won't be possible before 4:00 unless he asks for express service.

Development 创新

• Who should be responsible for the money left in the guest's pocket when a room attendant is collecting the laundry?

• How will the hotel make any compensation for the damage done in the laundry?

• If you can't find the guest's mis-delivered laundry, what should you do?

技能实训 13 客房送餐服务 Room Service

Section A

Basic Knowledge for Position 岗位基础知识

I. Word Stock 词库

steak sandwich	牛排三明治
club sandwich	总会三明治
black coffee	清咖啡
white coffee	奶咖啡
French fries	薯条
fruit salad	水果色拉
green salad	生菜色拉
dessert	甜点
thermal cupboard	保温柜
mutton curry	咖喱羊肉
snack	小吃
fried noodles	炒面
fresh juice	新鲜果汁
trolley	餐车

II. Pronunciation 语音训练

1. You may dial 8, then ask for room service.
   请您先拨 8，然后告诉送餐服务台。
2. Room service is available 24 hours every day.
   客房送餐服务全天 24 小时都提供。
3. Breakfast is served from 7:30 to 10:00 a.m., lunch and dinner served from 11:00 a.m. to 12:00 p.m.
   早餐从上午 7:30 供应到 10 点整，午餐和晚餐是从上午 11 点供应到晚上 12 点。
4. There is an extra service charge of 15% for room service.
   客房送餐服务要加收 15% 的服务费。
5. What kind of juice would you like, orange juice or papaya juice?
   您喜欢哪种果汁？橘子汁还是木瓜汁？

6. How would you like your eggs, soft boiled or hard boiled?
   您点的蛋要怎么做？煮得嫩一点还是老一点？

7. How would you like your steak to be cooked? Rare, medium or well-done?
   您点的牛排要怎么做？三分熟、五分熟还是全熟？

8. Would you prefer rolls or toast?
   您想要小圆面包还是烤面包？

9. May I have your name and room number please?
   请告诉我您的名字和房号好吗？

10. Shall I serve the soup, sir?
    先生，要我给您上汤吗？

11. Do you have a pen handy?
    您手边有笔吗？

12. I'm afraid there might be a short delay, madam. It's very busy today.
    对不起，女士，可能要等一会儿，今天特别忙。

13. Your food should be with you in twenty minutes, sir.
    先生，您的菜20分钟后可以送到。

14. Would you please call room service when you finish your meal, sir?
    先生，当您用完餐的时候请拨打送餐服务的电话。

Section B

Service Procedure 服务流程

1. Greetings.
   问候。

2. Ask the guest what would like to have.
   询问客人要点什么。

3. Ask the guest's name and room number.
   询问客人的名字和房号。

4. Make confirmation.
   确认。

5. Tell the guest how long it will take to prepare for the order.
   告诉客人需要多长时间送餐。

6. Deliver the food to the guest's room.
   送餐到客人的房间。

7. Speak out the order and give the bill to the guest.
   念一遍餐单，然后把账单给客人。

8. Ask the guest to sign his name and room number.
   请客人签上姓名和房号。

9. Express your wishes.
   表达祝愿。

Ⅰ. Service Performance 服务演练

G＝Guest（客人）　　　R＝Room Service Waiter（送餐服务员）

R：Good evening. Room service. Can I help you?
　　晚上好，送餐服务。您需要什么帮助吗？

G：Yes, It's Mr. Wang. May I order something to eat, please?
　　是的，我是王先生，我想点一些吃的东西，可以吗？

R：Of course, sir. May I have your room number?
　　当然可以，先生。请告诉我您的房号好吗？

G：My room number is 618.
　　我的房号是618。

R：What would you like to have, sir?
　　先生，您要点什么？

G：I'd like to have a plate of mutton curry.
　　我要一盘咖喱羊肉。

R：Er, I'm afraid it is not on our snack menu.
　　呃，不好意思，我们的小吃单上没有这个菜。

G：But it's on the room service menu.
　　可是客房服务菜单上有啊。

R：Yes, sir, but I'm afraid that the menu only applies to order up till midnight. It's one o'clock, sir.
　　是有，先生，可是那个菜单上的菜只供应到半夜。现在是1点钟了，先生。

G：Oh, OK. So what can I have, then?
　　哦，好的，那我能吃到什么呢？

R：We have a lot of toasted sandwiches and snack that you can choose.
　　我们有各种烤三明治和小吃供您选择。

G：Could you make me a club sandwich?
　　你们能给我来个总会三明治吗？

R：Yes, sir. And would you like a drink to go with that, sir?
　　当然可以，先生。您还要来点佐餐饮料吗？

G：Some black coffee, please.

来一壶清咖啡吧。

R：So that's a club sandwich and a pot of black coffee, sir?

那么您点的是一份总会三明治和一壶清咖啡，对吗？

G：Yes, that's right. When will it be ready?

对，没错。请问什么时候送到？

R：You should get it in about 15 minutes.

15分钟左右就能给您送去。

G：Fine. Thanks a lot. Goodbye.

好的，多谢。再见。

R：Goodbye.

再见。

Ⅱ. Position Practice 岗位实训

★ Taking room service orders over the phone.（受理送餐电话预订）

1. Could you send up a club sandwich, please?

   能送一个总会三明治过来吗？

2. Can you bring me up a plate of mutton curry, please?

   能否送一盘咖喱羊肉过来？

3. Could you do me a steak sandwich, please?

   能否给我做一个牛排三明治？

★ Checking and confirming a room service order.（核对和确认送餐菜单）

1. Can I just read that back to you, sir? That's a steak sandwich and a beer. Is that correct, sir?

   我把它报给您听一下好吗？一份牛排三明治和一瓶啤酒，对吗？

2. I'll just read it back to you, sir. That's a fried noodles and an orange juice. Is that right, sir?

   先生，我报给您听一下。一份炒面和一杯橙汁，对吗？

3. So that's a club sandwich and a pot of white coffee, madam?

   女士，您点的是一个总会三明治和一壶奶咖啡，对吗？

★ Apologizing in advance.（先行致歉）

1. I'm terribly sorry, but we only serve local drinks, sir.

   先生，很抱歉，我们只供应当地的饮料。

2. I'm afraid it is not on the menu, madam.

   女士，这个东西恐怕不在菜单上。

3. I'm afraid the room service is not in operation, sir.

   先生，恐怕送餐服务现在暂停了。

4. I'm terribly sorry, sir, but there is no electricity at the moment.
   很抱歉，先生，现在没电。

★ Delivering food to rooms.（送餐进房间）

1. Where can I put the tray, sir?
   先生，请问托盘放在哪儿？
2. Shall I serve it now or shall I leave it in the thermal cupboard?
   要我现在就端出来还是把它放在保温柜里？
3. Would you please sign the bill, please?
   麻烦您把账单签一下好吗？
4. If you prefer, you can leave the tray outside.
   如果您愿意，可以把托盘放在门外。

Ⅲ. Listening Practice 听力实训

★ A. Listen to the conversation and take room service orders.

```
                    Paris Palace Hotel
                    Room Service Orders
  Room Number _____
  Guest's Name _____
  Order
  _____
  _____
  _____
  _____
  Taken by _____
```

★ B. Complete the following dialogue.

Room Service：Room Service.

Guest：Come in please.

Room Service：Thank you, madam. _____?

Guest：Yes, sure.

Room Service：_____?

Guest：Yes, that's right. That looks great.

Room service：_____?

Guest：OK! Do you have a pen handy?

Room Service：Here you are, madam.

Guest：Thanks... OK?

Room Service: Yes, madam. _____? They'll come and collect the tray.

Guest: Thank you. I'll do that.

Room Service: Goodbye, madam. _____.

Guest: Thank you. Goodbye.

Important 特别关注

▲ The guest can get the room service by telephone or by doorknob menu.
客人可以通过电话或者填写门把菜单来获得客房送餐服务。

▲ If there is a minimum charge or service charge, you have to explain it to the guest clearly in advance.
如果有最低消费或服务费，跟客人提前说清楚。

▲ Sometimes room service waiters serve cocktail parties or dinner in the guest rooms. They are salesmen as well as waiters.
有时候送餐服务员还会在客人的房间里给客人举办鸡尾酒会或送晚餐。他们既可以是销售人员也可以是服务员。

Section C

Case and Development 案例与创新

Case 案例

Mr. Roberts in Room 605 wants to order two steaks with French fries and a bottle of red wine. The clerk of room service answers the phone and accepts the order. She assures the guest the order will be ready in 20 minutes. The room attendant sends the order to the guest's room and asks him to sign the bill.

Development 创新

• To which department does the room service belong?

• Do you think it is necessary to tell the guest how long it will take to deliver food to his room?

• What shall you ask the guest to do when he wants to add the cost of room service to the room bill?

技能实训 14 维修服务 Maintenance Service

听力音频

Section A

Basic Knowledge for Position 岗位基础知识

I. Word Stock 词库

faucet	水龙头
furniture	家具
washing basin	洗脸盆
mirror	镜子
curtain	窗帘
blanket	毛毯
drawer	抽屉
broadband	宽带
bedside light	床头灯
floor lamp	地灯
table lamp	台灯
mini bar	小冰箱
electric kettle	电开水壶
fax machine	传真机
air conditioner	空调
central air heating/conditioning	中央供暖/空调
smoke sensor	烟感器
safety deposit box	保险柜
bedside control panel	床头控制板

II. Pronunciation 语音训练

1. I'm very annoyed. My TV isn't working.
   我很恼火，我的电视机坏了。

2. I'm very annoyed. There are no towels in the bathroom.
   我很恼火，卫生间里没有毛巾。

3. The room is just not good enough. There's a large pool of water on the floor.
   这房间可真差劲，地板上有一大摊水。

4. There's a terrible smell in my bathroom.
   我的卫生间里有一股难闻的气味。

5. The air conditioner/heating system isn't working.
   空调/暖气坏了。

6. I'm very sorry. I'll make sure the room attendant will clean your room at once.
   真抱歉，我一定马上让客房服务员打扫您的房间。

7. I'm terribly sorry. I'll send an engineer up soon.
   非常抱歉，我马上派工程师来。

8. Please look into it and carry out repairs as soon as possible.
   请尽快调查并进行修理。

9. I'll have someone fix them for you right away.
   我马上派人给您修理。

10. I'll ask the maintenance department to look into it at once.
    我马上叫维修部派人来检查。

11. We do apologize for the inconvenience.
    我们很抱歉给您带来不便。

12. It takes time to repair. I'm afraid you have to change to another room.
    修理需要一些时间。恐怕您得换个房间了。

Section B

Service Procedure 服务流程

1. Greetings.
   问候。

2. Listen to what the guest says patiently.
   耐心听客人述说。

3. Make apologies to the guest and get the guest's room number.
   向客人道歉并问清房号。

4. Tell the guest what measures will be done immediately.
   告知客人马上要采取的对策。

5. Inform the maintenance department to repair at once.
   马上通知维修部进行修理。

6. Repairman comes to offer service for the guest.
   维修人员上门服务。
7. Apologize and repair.
   道歉并进行维修。
8. Tell the guest that the problem has been solved.
   告诉客人问题解决了。
9. Express good wishes to the guest.
   表达祝愿。

Ⅰ. Service Performance 服务演练

R = Room Attendant（客房服务员）　　G = Guest（客人）　　E = Electrician（电工）

R：Good afternoon, sir. What can I do for you?
   先生，下午好，能够为您做什么？
G：I'm afraid there's something wrong with the TV. The picture is wobbling.
   我的电视机恐怕出问题了，图像在晃动。
R：I'm sorry, sir. May I have your room number?
   先生，很抱歉，请告知您的房号好吗？
G：Yes, Room 815, Mr. White.
   好的，815房间，怀特先生。
R：I'll inform the maintenance department at once. We can have it repaired. Please wait just a few minutes, Mr. White.
   我马上通知维修部。怀特先生，我们能修好的，请稍等几分钟。
   (Five minutes later, there is a knock on the door.)（五分钟之后，有人敲门。）
E：Maintenance, may I come in?
   维修部，可以进来吗？
G：(Opening the door) Yes, please.
   （打开门）请进吧。
E：Hello, Mr. White. The TV set is not working well, is it?
   您好，怀特先生。电视机不能正常工作是吗？
G：No, it isn't.
   是的，坏了。
E：Let me check it. (He finishes the repairing.) Mr. White, everything is OK now. Is there anything else I can do for you?
   让我检查一下。（检修完毕后）怀特先生，都修好了，还有什么需要我做的吗？
G：No, thanks. How efficient you are! (Taking out some money.) This is for you.
   没有了，谢谢。你们的效率真高。（拿出一些钱）这是给你的。

E：Oh, no. We won't accept tips, but thank you anyway. We wish you a nice stay with us.
哦，我们不收小费的，但还是谢谢您。祝您在这儿过得愉快！

Ⅱ. Position Practice 岗位实训

★ Four categories of Maintenance. （维修的四种类型）

1. Preventive room maintenance 预防性房间保养
2. Preventive equipment maintenance 预防性设备保养
3. Routine repairs based on work-orders 按工作程序的日常维修
4. Emergencies 紧急事件

★ Emergency notice. （紧急通知）

May I have your attention, please? This is emergent. The hotel is on fire now. Please leave your room immediately and follow the emergency exist. Please leave this building immediately. Thank you for your cooperation.

紧急事故，请注意！酒店发生火灾。请立刻离开房间，从紧急出口撤离。请马上离开酒店。谢谢您的合作。

★ About Emergency Exit. （关于紧急出口）

When a guest has checked in and been escorted by a bellman to his room, he should first look for information in his room about fire safety and location of nearest fire exits. How many doors away? Does the door open easily? Are the fire exit signs illuminated? If the lights are off, contact the front desk to let them know.

当客人在酒店登记入住并由行李员带到房间后，他应该立刻寻找他的房间里关于消防安全的信息并确定最近的逃生通道。看看逃生通道距离自己的房间有几扇门？逃生通道的门容易打开吗？紧急出口的标识亮着吗？如果灯光熄灭了，一定要通知前台。

★ How to use the safety deposit box in the room. （怎样使用房间内的保险箱）

First open the safe. When "Open" is showed, you must set the code by inputting six-digit password. Then you can put your valuables inside and close the safe. At that time "Lock" will be showed. Remember your password you set otherwise it will cause you much trouble.

首先打开保险箱。当显示"Open"字样时，您得输入六位阿拉伯数字来设定密码。然后您将贵重物品放入并关上门，这时会出现"Lock"字样。您千万要记住自己设置的密码，否则就麻烦了。

Ⅲ. Listening Practice 听力实训

★ A. Listen to the recording and complete the conversation.

Repairman：(Knocking at the door.) _____?
Guest：Yes, come in please.

Repairman: Good afternoon, sir. _____?

Guest: The air-conditioner doesn't work, it is terribly hot.

Repairman: I'm sorry, sir. Let me have a look. Oh, _____. I'll change one for you.

Guest: Thank you. By the way, there is something wrong with the faucet. I can't turn off the faucet above the washbasin.

Repairman: _____.

Guest: How long shall I have to wait?

Repairman: About fifteen minutes.

Guest: OK.

Repairman: Everything is all right, sir. _____.

Guest: That's OK. Thank you very much.

★ B. Listen to the recording and make out what a room attendant should do and what a repairman should do. Write "RA" for room attendant, write "R" for repairman.

1. Making beds in guest rooms. (   )
2. Changing a burnt-out light bulb in a lamp in the guest room. (   )
3. Polishing the guest's leather shoes. (   )
4. Sending another pair of slippers to the guest room. (   )
5. Air conditioners must be cleaned or replaced regularly. (   )
6. Be responsible for electrical and plumbing systems. (   )
7. Guest is ill and sends him for a doctor. (   )
8. Mini bar in the guest room is out of order. (   )

Important 特别关注

▲ Report any problems which require repair or maintenance as soon as you observe them.
看到任何需要维修或保养的问题都要及时反映。

▲ Safety means preventing accidents which can harm both employees and guests.
安全就意味着要防止任何危害员工和客人的事故发生。

▲ Accidents are caused by carelessness; they are unplanned and unforeseen.
事故是由粗心导致的, 它们无法计划, 也无法预料。

▲ A lack of preventive maintenance and attention to detail is the major cause many emergencies.
缺少保养、忽视细节是导致紧急事件发生的真正原因。

▲ In case of fire or other accidents, keep calm and inform the front desk immediately, then evacuate through fire escape.
如果发生火灾或其他意外事件时, 请您不要惊慌, 立即通知前台, 并按安全疏散

路线迅速撤离。

▲ The chief maintenance engineer must be willing to respond to emergencies, even if off work.
维修总工程师必须对紧急事件立即做出反应,哪怕是在他下班之后。

Section C

Case and Development 案例与创新

Case 案例

You are a guest. You are not satisfied with your room. The air conditioner is too noisy. You'd like the room attendant to change a room for you.

You are a room attendant. You listen carefully to the guest's complaint and make a note of that. You apologize to him and phone the reception desk to see if there is room available. You promise to have the room repaired at once. Repairman will arrive in five minutes.

Development 创新

• What are the duties of the maintenance department staff?

• How do you understand the saying about emergencies — "your poor planning is becoming my crisis"?

• What are the new challenges that the maintenance department face nowadays?

实训模块四

餐饮服务
Food and Beverage

The food and beverage service is the second major activity of most hotels. In contrast with the Housing Department, the Food and Beverage Department needs to hire more people. This is because the Food and Beverage Department serves not only the in-house guests but also non-in-house guests, and it is a relatively labor-intensive department.

餐饮服务是大部分酒店的第二主业,比起客房部,餐饮部需要雇用更多的人手。这是因为酒店的餐饮部在招待住店客人的同时,也接待非住店客人,而且它是相对劳动密集型的部门。

技能实训 15　餐台预订 Reservations

Section A
Basic Knowledge for Position 岗位基础知识

I. Word Stock 词库

Chinese Restaurant	中餐厅
Western Restaurant	西餐厅
waiter/waitress	男侍应生/女侍应生
Korean Cuisine	韩国菜
Japanese Cuisine	日本菜
Tai Cuisine	泰国菜
Chinese food/Western food	中餐/西餐
speciality restaurant	风味餐厅
tea house	茶室
cafe	咖啡馆
snack bar	小吃吧
cafeteria	自助式餐厅
excluding drinks	不包含酒水
including drinks	包含酒水
minimum consumption	最低消费
recommend	介绍
cuisine	菜谱，菜系
off season	淡季
peak season	旺季
guarantee	保证

II. Pronunciation 语音训练

1. What time would you like your table, sir?
   先生，您想订什么时间的座位？

2. For how many people?
   一共有多少人？

3. Would you like a table in the hall or in a private room?
   您是喜欢大厅的餐台还是包间呢？

4. At what time will you arrive here?
   您预计几点光临？

5. I'm afraid we are fully booked for that time.
   恐怕那个时间段的座位已经订满了。

6. Would you like to be put on the waiting list?
   您愿意被列入等候名单吗？

7. Let me check if there is a vacancy.
   我查一下是否还有空位。

8. Just a moment please. I'll check the reservation record for you.
   请稍候，我看一下预订记录。

9. May I have your name and telephone number, please?
   请告诉我您的名字和电话号码好吗？

10. So that's a table for 10 on Sunday evening, is that right?
    您订的是周日晚上的 10 个人的座位，对吗？

11. Thank you for calling. We're expecting to serve you soon.
    谢谢来电，我们期待着为您服务。

12. The minimum charge for a private room is 200 yuan per person.
    包厢最低消费是每人 200 元。

Section B

Service Procedure 服务流程

1. Greetings.
   问候。

2. Ask the information about table reservation, such as the date, number of people, arrival time, the guest's name and telephone number etc.
   询问预订信息，诸如就餐日期、人数、抵达时间、客人的名字和联系电话等。

3. Make confirmation about reservation.
   确认预订。

4. Express your expectation to the guest.
   表达期待客人的光临。

I. Service Performance 服务演练

C＝Reservation Clerk（预订人员）　　G＝Guest（客人）

C：Good morning, Black Rose Restaurant. Can I help you?
　早上好，黑玫瑰餐厅。能够为您做什么？

G：Yes, I'd like to book a table for dinner.
　我想订座。

C：Certainly. What time would you like your table?
　好的。请问您什么时间用餐？

G：This Saturday evening.
　本周六晚上。

C：How large a group are you?
　你们一共有多少个人？

G：Six couples.
　六对夫妇。

C：Just a moment please, sir. I'll check the reservation record for you.
　请稍等，先生。我查一下预订记录。

G：May I have a private room?
　我能够订一间包厢吗？

C：I'm afraid not, sir. All the private rooms are occupied. Would you like to have a table in the hall?
　恐怕不行，先生。所有的包厢都订满了。订一张大厅的桌子行吗？

G：OK. Would you do me a favor to book a table a little bit quiet?
　好吧。你能否帮忙订一个安静点的位置？

C：Sure. I'll book the table by the window for you.
　当然可以。我把靠窗户的位置给您。

G：Thank you.
　谢谢。

C：And what time can we expect you, sir?
　先生，你们什么时候到达餐厅？

G：At about 6 o'clock.
　大约6点钟。

C：May I have your name and telephone number?

请告诉我您的名字和电话号码。

G：My name is Ron Kollitz, K-O-L-L-I-T-Z, and my telephone number is 33956678555.

我叫罗恩·科里茨，K-O-L-L-I-T-Z，我的电话是 33956678555。

C：Thank you. So that's a table for six couples in the name of Mr. Kollitz on Saturday evening, your phone number is 33956678555, is that right?

谢谢！科里茨先生预订本周六晚上一个 12 人的座位，您的电话号码是 33956678555，对吗？

G：Yes, that's right.

没错。

C：Thank you for your calling. We're looking forward to serving you soon.

谢谢您的来电。我们期待为您服务。

Ⅱ. Position Practice 岗位实训

★ Four different reservations.（四种不同的预订方式）

1. Face to face reservation.

   面对面预订。

2. Telephone reservation.

   电话预订。

3. Fax reservation.

   传真预订。

4. Internet reservation.

   网上预订。

In whatever way the reservation is made by the guest, you are supposed to confirm the following information about the arrival time, the number of the guests, the name and telephone number of the person who makes the reservation.

无论客人用何种方式预订用餐，你都要确认以下信息：客人抵达餐厅的时间、用餐的人数、预订人的姓名和电话号码。

★ Banquet reservation.（宴会预订）

1. May I know what the banquet is for?

   请问这个宴会是什么类型的？

2. How much would you like to spend for each person?

   请问每个人的用餐标准是多少？

3. How would you like us to lay out the banquet?

   您想要我们怎么布置宴会呢？

4. There's a minimum charge of 3000 yuan for each table.
   每桌餐最低消费 3000 元。

5. Is there anything special you'd like to have on the menu?
   您对菜单有什么特殊要求？

6. How would you like to make payment, madam?
   女士，请问您用何种方式付款？

7. We'll fax the banquet menu and details to you tomorrow.
   明天我们把菜单和宴会细节传真给您。

★ Refuse a reservation politely. （婉拒预订）

1. I'm afraid we're fully booked for tonight.
   很抱歉，今天晚上全部预订满了。

2. Would you like to make a reservation at another restaurant in our hotel?
   您是否愿意在我们饭店的另一家餐厅订餐？

3. Shall I transfer your call, madam?
   女士，我可以把您的电话转接过去吗？

4. Would you like to be put on the waiting list?
   您愿意被列入等候名单吗？

★ Giving information about restaurant. （告知营业信息）

1. We are open all round the clock.
   我们 24 个小时营业。

2. We are open until 10:00 p.m., but our last order for dinner is at 9:00 p.m.
   我们一直营业到晚上 10 点，但晚餐点菜的截止时间是晚上 9 点。

3. We serve a great variety of popular Chinese dishes in table d'hote and a la carte.
   我们供应各种各样的中国名菜，有套餐也可以零点。

Ⅲ. Listening Practice 听力实训

★ A. Listen to the recording, decide what each short dialogue is about and mark "√" where appropriate.

	Bar	Cafe	Restaurant	Cafeteria	Banquet Hall
Dialogue 1					
Dialogue 2					
Dialogue 3					
Dialogue 4					
Dialogue 5					

★ B. Complete the following conversation.

Reservationist: Babylon Hotel. Can I help you?

Caller: Yes. Could I make a booking at the Bay view Restaurant?

Reservationist: Certainly, madam. _____?

Caller: It's for me and my husband on Friday 23rd.

Reservationist: _____ on Friday 23rd. Under whose name please?

Caller: Hudson.

Reservationist: Ms. Hudson. Thank you, madam. _____?

Caller: 7:30.

Reservationist: _____. That's a table for two at 7:30 on Friday 23rd _____.

Caller: Yes, that's correct.

Reservationist: Thank you very much, Ms. Hudson.

Caller: Thank you. Goodbye.

Reservationist: Goodbye.

Important 特别关注

▲ If the restaurant has minimum charge, you should make it clear in advance to the person who makes the reservation.
如果餐厅有最低消费,要事先跟预订人说清楚。

▲ For a large-scale or an important banquet reservation, a face to face talk is suggested.
如果是大规模或重要的宴会预订,建议与预订人面对面商谈。

Section C

Case and Development 案例与创新

Case 案例

Guest: You would like to book a table for 6 in Maya Restaurant of Hong Xing Hotel on Saturday evening. You want the table in the non-smoking area with the window seat. And a baby seat is also needed.

Reservation Clerk: You answer the phone on Thursday afternoon, and put down the reservation as required.

Development 创新

- If your restaurant is fully booked for the time the guest wants to reserve, what would you say to him? what kind of suggestions do you usually make?
- Will you repeat the reservation for confirmation, why or why not?
- If it is a banquet reservation, what are the main points you have to make sure?

技能实训 16　餐厅迎客服务 Receiving Diners

听力音频

Section A

Basic Knowledge for Position 岗位基础知识

I. Word Stock 词库

individual	散客；零星的
diner	就餐者
head waiter, head waitress	领班
supervisor	主管
smoking area	吸烟区
non-smoking area	非吸烟区
arrange	安排
meal voucher	餐券
extra	额外的，另加的
food and beverage manager	餐饮部经理
catering/banquet manager	宴会厅经理
restaurant supervisor	餐厅主管

II. Pronunciation 语音训练

1. Good evening. Welcome to our restaurant.
   晚上好，欢迎光临！
2. Do you have a reservation, sir?
   先生，请问您有预订吗？
3. How many, please?
   一共几位？
4. Are there only two of you?
   就你们两位吗？
5. May I have your name and phone number?
   可以告诉我您的名字和电话号码吗？
6. Just a moment please, I'll check the record.
   请稍等，我查一下记录。

7. Yes, a table for two under the name of Bill Smith.
   是的，比尔·史密斯订的两个人的座位。

8. Follow me, please.
   请跟我来。

9. Would you like to sit by the window?
   您喜欢靠窗户的位置吗?

10. Yes, we have booked a table for you.
    是的，我们给您预订了一张桌子。

11. Will this table be all right for you, madam?
    女士，这个座位可以吗?

12. I'm afraid that table has been booked.
    恐怕这个座位已经被预订了。

13. Take your time, please.
    请慢慢来。

14. A waiter will come to take your order.
    服务生会过来给您点单。

15. Would you mind sharing a table?
    您介意拼桌吗?

16. It's rather busy at the moment.
    现在很忙。

17. Sorry, the restaurant is full. Would you like to try some Western food?
    对不起，本餐厅已满座。您能否改为品尝西餐?

Section B

Service Procedure 服务流程

1. Greetings.
   问候。

2. Ask the guest whether he has a reservation.
   询问客人是否有预订。

3. Check the reservation record if there is a reservation.
   如果有预订，查一下预订记录。

4. Arrange a table for a guest without a reservation.
   给没有预订的客人安排座位。

5. Show the way.
   给客人带路。
6. Ask the guest to take a seat.
   安排客人入座。
7. Inform the guest the waiter will be with him soon.
   告知客人服务生很快就到。

Ⅰ. Service Performance 服务演练

H＝Hostess（迎宾员）　　G＝Guest（客人）

H: Good evening, ladies and gentlemen. Welcome to our restaurant. Are you of the same group?
   晚上好，女士们、先生们，欢迎光临。你们是一起的吗？
G: Yes, we are. We have a reservation in your restaurant.
   是的。我们有预订。
H: May I know who made the reservation, please?
   请告诉我是谁预订的好吗？
G: Mr. Thompson.
   汤普森先生。
H: OK. Let me have a check. Yes, your table is in private room 615. This way, please.
   好的，我查一下。是的，你们的座位在615包厢。请这边走。
G: Thank you.
   谢谢。
H: Will this table be all right?
   这个座位行吗？
G: I think so.
   可以。
H: Please take your seats.
   请坐。
G: Are the drinks included in the minimum charge?
   请问酒水含在最低消费中吗？
H: No, I'm afraid you'll have to pay extra for drinks.
   不含在最低消费，您得另外付酒水的费用。
G: Yes, I will. I'd like to have a look at the menu.
   好的，我想看看菜单。
H: Just a moment, please. Here is the menu. You can choose what you like from the menu. The waitress will take your order later.
   请稍等。这是菜单，您可以随便选，服务生过一会儿为您点单。

G：Thanks a lot.
多谢。

H：You're welcome. I hope you will enjoy your meal.
不客气，希望你们在这儿用餐愉快！

Ⅱ. Position Practice 岗位实训

★ Telling the guest there isn't a table.（告诉客人餐厅客满）

1. I'm sorry, there aren't any tables available... would you please wait in the waiting room?
   很抱歉，现在没有座位了，您愿意在等候室等一会儿吗？

2. I'm sorry, the restaurant is full now.
   很抱歉，餐厅满座了。

3. We can seat you in 15 minutes.
   我们可以在15分钟之后给您安排座位。

4. Would you like to have a drink in the lounge while you wait? We'll seat you as soon as possible.
   您愿意在休息室喝杯东西等一会儿吗？我们将尽快安排你们入座。

★ Receiving guests with a reservation.（迎接有预订的客人）

1. Do you have a reservation?
   请问您有预订吗？

2. May I have your name, please?
   请问您贵姓？

3. I'm afraid the table you reserved is not ready yet.
   恐怕您预订的餐桌还没有准备好。

4. We're expecting you.
   我们正在恭候您的光临。

★ Arranging the table for the guest.（给客人安排餐桌）

1. Would you mind sharing a table?
   您介意和别人拼桌吗？

2. Would you mind sitting separately?
   你们是否介意分开坐？

3. I'm afraid that table is reserved.
   恐怕那个座位已经有人预订了。

4. Would you prefer smoking area or non-smoking area?
   您想坐在吸烟区还是无烟区？

Ⅲ. Listening Practice 听力实训

★ A. Listen to the conversation and tell different features of four main cuisines.

Four Main Cuisines	Features
Guangdong Cuisine	
Sichuan Cuisine	
Shandong Cuisine	
Huaiyang Cuisine	

★ B. Complete the following conversation.

Clerk：Good evening，sir. Welcome to our restaurant.
Diner：Good evening. I'd like a table for five，please.
Clerk：_____?
Diner：No，I'm afraid not.
Clerk：This way，please.
...
Clerk：_____?
Diner：Well，I prefer a table by the window.
Clerk：I'm sorry，but all the _____.
Diner：Oh，I see. We'll have to make up with this one.
Clerk：_____.
Diner：Can we smoke?
Clerk：Sorry，this is _____.
Diner：OK.
Clerk：Hers is the menu. _____.
Have a good appetite!
Diner：Thank you.

Important 特别关注

▲To avoid making guests feel embarrassed and unpleasant，you should explain it to the guests politely if there are special clothing requirements in some luxury hotels.
有的高档餐厅对客人有着装上的要求，这时要向客人礼貌地说明，以免造成尴尬和不快。

▲In formal Western banquets，couples are usually not arranged to sit together to avoid small talks and consequently neglect of communication with other guests.
在西餐正式宴会中，一般不安排夫妻坐在一起，以免各自聊家常而忽略与其他宾客

的交流。

Section C

Case and Development 案例与创新

Case 案例

Guest：You come into a crowded restaurant. You haven't made any reservation. You don't like the table the hostess offers you, because it's too close to the toilet. You don't mind sharing a table with other people.

Hostess：You greet the guest and seat him. If he doesn't like the table near the toilet, ask him if he minds sharing a table with other people.

Development 创新

- What's the job of a hostess? Who also greets and sends off the guest?
- What should be kept in mind when a hostess arranges seats?
- What can you do for the guest if there is an overbooking in your restaurant?

技能实训 17 中餐厅服务
At a Chinese Restaurant

Section A

Basic Knowledge for Position 岗位基础知识

I. Word Stock 词库

Shandong cuisine	鲁菜
Guangdong cuisine	粤菜
Sichuan cuisine	川菜
Hunan cuisine	湘菜
Huaiyang cuisine	淮扬菜
Zhejiang cuisine	浙江菜
Fujian cuisine	闽菜
Anhui cuisine	徽菜
boil	水煮
steam	蒸
braise	焖
stir	炒
fry	煎
deep fry	炸
smoke	烟熏
roast	烤
stew	煨，炖
bake	烘焙
cure	腌制
barbecue	烧烤
rice wine	米酒
ginger	生姜
garlic	大蒜
shallot	葱
vinegar	醋

soy sauce	酱油
salt	盐
pepper	胡椒
sugar	糖

🔊 Ⅱ. Pronunciation 语音训练

1. Many guests give high comments on Maotai.
   许多宾客对茅台酒赞赏有加。

2. It never goes to the head.
   （不管喝多少）它都不上头。

3. I suggest that you have a taste of Sichuan cuisine.
   我建议你们尝尝川菜。

4. Try the green crab if you don't mind.
   如果您不介意的话，不妨尝一下青蟹。

5. You'll regret if you don't have a taste.
   如果您不尝一下，您准会后悔的。

6. It's delicious and worth a try.
   它鲜美可口，值得一试。

7. I'm sorry to have kept you waiting.
   很抱歉，让您久等了。

8. I'm really sorry, but I seem to have served a wrong dish.
   真对不起，我好像上错了一个菜。

9. I do apologize for giving you the wrong soup.
   我上错汤了，真抱歉。

10. Please feel free to contact us if you have any questions.
    如果您有什么问题，请随时和我们联系。

11. How do you like the fish cooked this way?
    您觉得鱼这样烧怎么样？

12. What do you think of Chinese food?
    您认为中国菜怎么样？

13. Do you think the soup is tasty?
    您认为这个汤可口吗？

14. What's your opinion of their service?
    您对他们的服务有什么意见吗？

Section B

Serivce Procedure 服务流程

1. Greetings.
   问候。
2. Offer tea.
   上茶。
3. Take orders and serve dishes.
   点菜、上菜。
4. Service during the meals.
   餐间服务。
5. Dessert and fruits.
   上甜品、水果。
6. Settle the bill.
   结账。
7. Bid farewell to the guests.
   送客。

Ⅰ. Service Performance 服务演练

W＝Waitress（服务生）　　　G＝Guest（客人）

W：Good evening, sir. Would you like some green tea?
　　晚上好，先生。喝点绿茶吗？

G：Yes, please.
　　好的。

W：Are you ready to order now, sir?
　　先生，准备好点菜了吗？

G：Yes. But this is our first visit to China. We love Chinese food, but we know very little about it.
　　是的。但这是我们第一次来中国。我们喜欢中国菜，但对它一无所知。

W：Well, there are eight main cuisines in China, such as Guangdong cuisine, Sichuan cuisine and Zhejiang cuisine…
　　嗯，中国有八大菜系，如粤菜、川菜、浙江菜……

G：How is Zhejiang cuisine different from Sichuan cuisine?
　　浙江菜与川菜有何不同？

W：Zhejiang cuisine tends to be fresh and mild while most Sichuan cuisine are spicy and hot.

浙江菜比较温和、新鲜，而川菜比较麻和辣。

G：That sounds great, we'd like to try some Zhejiang cuisine.
听起来不错，我们想尝尝浙江菜。

W：Yes, sure.
好的。

G：Let's have Shelled Shrimps with Longjing Tea leaves, please.
我们要龙井虾仁。

W：It's one of the famous dishes of Zhejiang. It looks nice both in shape and color, it is very delicious.
这是很有名的浙江菜之一，色香味俱全。

G：And what else do you recommend?
你还推荐什么菜？

W：Beggar's Chicken and Dongpo Pork are also typical dishes.
叫花鸡和东坡肉也是很经典的菜。

G：OK, we'd like to have a try.
好的，我们尝尝。

W：What about vegetables and soup?
来点什么蔬菜和汤呢？

G：Broccoli and mushroom soup, please.
来点西兰花和蘑菇汤吧。

W：So you order Shelled Shrimps with Longjing Tea leaves, Beggar's, Chicken and Dongpo Pork, broccoli and mushroom soup, is that right?
您点了龙井虾仁、叫花鸡、东坡肉、西兰花和蘑菇汤，对吗？

G：Yes, that's right!
是的，没错。

W：Your dishes will be ready in 15 minutes.
您的菜15分钟后上。

G：OK.
好的。

(15 minutes later.)（15分钟之后。）

W：This is Shelled Shrimps with Longjing Tea leaves, enjoy your meal.
这是您点的龙井虾仁，请慢用。

G：Thank you.
谢谢。

W：That's all for your dishes. If you need anything else, please let us know.
您的菜上齐了，如果还有什么需要请告诉我们。

G：Sure.

没问题。

W：May I take your plate away, please?

能够把您的餐盘换一下吗?

G：Yes, thank you.

好的, 谢谢。

W：Enjoy your meal, please.

请慢用。

G：Waitress, bill, please.

服务生, 买单。

W：Yes, the total is 350 yuan. How would you like to make payment, sir?

好的, 总共是 350 元。您要怎么付款?

G：By cash, please.

现金付款吧。

W：OK, this is your receipt. Thank you for coming and we are looking forward to serving you again.

好的, 这是您的收据, 谢谢光临, 期待再次为您服务。

G：Good bye.

再见。

Ⅱ. Position Practice 岗位实训

★ Characteristics of Chinese cuisines. （中国菜系的特征）

Chinese food has many cuisines. In the Qing Dynasty, Chinese food formed four major cuisines, namely Shandong cuisine, Sichuan cuisine, Guangdong cuisine, and Huaiyang cuisine. Later, Fujian cuisine, Zhejiang cuisine, Hunan cuisine, and Anhui cuisine became increasingly popular, thus forming China's "eight major cuisines".

中国的菜肴有许多菜系。在清代, 中国菜形成了鲁菜、川菜、粤菜、淮扬菜四大菜系, 后来闽菜、浙江菜、湘菜、徽菜等也逐渐出名, 于是形成了中国的 "八大菜系"。

★ Introduce soft drinks (drinks without alcohol). ［向客人介绍软饮料（不含酒精的饮料）］

juice 果汁

black coffee 清咖啡

white coffee 奶咖啡

green tea 绿茶

black tea 红茶

brick tea 砖茶

flower tea 花茶

soda water 苏打水

mineral water 矿泉水

Coca Cola 可口可乐

Pepsi Cola 百事可乐

Sprite 雪碧

Fanta 芬达

★ Introduce different kinds of juice.（向客人介绍不同种类的果汁）

orange juice 橙汁

apple juice 苹果汁

watermelon juice 西瓜汁

lemon juice 柠檬汁

kiwi juice 猕猴桃汁

papaya juice 木瓜汁

coconut juice 椰子汁

cucumber juice 黄瓜汁

tomato juice 番茄汁

corn juice 玉米汁

★ Introduce some famous types of wine to guests.（向客人介绍几种著名的中国酒）

Wuliangye is a typical representative of Chinese Baijiu with a high degree of alcohol, but never easy to go to the head.

五粮液是中国白酒的典型代表，度数较高，但不容易上头。

Maotai is one of the three famous distilled liquors in the world along with Scotch whisky and French cognac. It is over 800 years old.

茅台酒是与苏格兰威士忌、法国科涅克白兰地齐名的世界三大蒸馏名酒之一。它已有800多年的历史。

Great Wall wine is a national brand of Chinese wine, which produced the first bottle of dry red, dry white, and traditional sparkling wine in China.

长城葡萄酒是中国葡萄酒的国家品牌，生产出了中国第一瓶干红、干白和传统法起泡葡萄酒。

Swellfun has a history of more than 600 years. It is full of traditional and cultural flavor, and has the purest nature with simplest style.

水井坊拥有600多年的历史，纯正、自然、简约，有极其深厚的文化底蕴。

Fenjiu Liquor has a history of over 1500 years. It is sparkling and crystal clear, pure and refreshing, and delicious with a delicate aroma.

汾酒拥有1500多年的历史，晶莹纯净，清新芳香，十分诱人。

Tsingtao is No. 1 beer brand in China, founded in 1903.

青岛啤酒是中国啤酒的第一品牌，创建于1903年。

Ⅲ. Listening Practice 听力实训

★ A. Listen to the short passage about snacks and fill in the missing words.

Snacks can be _____ in every city and all over the city. Steamed buns, wonton and other _____ can be seen everywhere in China. If you are _____, you can have a beer from a corner beer shop, and _____ you may try a small dish of peanuts. If you are in South, it's worth _____ at least one meal in dim sum restaurant. In the North you _____ go to a "small snack" restaurant. This is _____ people meet, from morning until afternoon, to _____ the latest news or even to discuss business. These restaurants are usually large, _____ and always bring happiness to the guests.

★ B. Complete the following conversation.

Hostess: _____, sir and madam?

Man: Yes, please. First, a Beijing roast duck.

Woman: I overheard that steamed Mandarin fish is very nice.

Hostess: Yes, _____.

Man: What kind of soup can you recommend?

Hostess: I'd like you to try mushroom soup, _____.

Woman: OK. And some green beans, please.

Hostess: _____?

Man: No, that's all.

Hostess: _____ a Beijing roast duck, steamed Mandarin fish, mushroom soup and green beans, is that right?

Woman: Yes, that's right. How long will it take?

Hostess: About 20 minutes. _____, sir and madam?

Man: Yes, a bottle of red wine, Dynasty, please.

Hostess: OK. Just a minute.

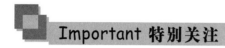

▲ Closely watch personal hygiene, wash hands before beginning work, and wash again after doing messy work.
密切关注个人卫生，开始工作前或干过脏活后都要洗手。

▲ No jewellery, rings, bracelets or wristwatches.
不佩戴珠宝、戒指、手镯或手表。

▲ Neatly dressed, short hair or updo. Well-groomed beards.
衣着整洁，留短发或把头发盘起来，胡须要修理干净。

▲ Solid working shoes with non-slippery soles.
穿鞋底防滑的牢固的工作鞋。

Section C

Case and Development 案例与创新

Case 案例

Waiter: You receive a couple who come to celebrate their 30th marriage anniversary. You congratulate them and make a few suggestions on Chinese food. You take the order and serve the dishes.

Guest: You are Mr. and Mrs. Tylor. You are on vacation in China. Today is your 30th marriage anniversary, and you want to have something different.

Development 创新

• Have Chinese eating habits changed a lot, why or why not?

• How can you teach the foreigners to use the chopsticks?

• Can you tell foreigners about some Chinese food like noodles or eggs which have symbolic meaning?

技能实训 18 西餐厅服务
At a Western Restaurant

听力音频

Section A

Basic Knowledge for Position 岗位基础知识

Ⅰ. Word Stock 词库

steak house	牛排馆
a la carte	零点；照单点菜
table d'hote	套餐
coffee shop/café	咖啡馆
menu	菜单
French/Italian cuisine	法国/意大利菜
continental cuisine	欧式西餐
today's special	今日特餐
chef's special	主厨特餐
buffet	自助餐
fast food	快餐
specialty	招牌菜
aperitif	开胃酒
French fries	炸薯条
baked potato	烘马铃薯
mashed potato	土豆泥
pudding	布丁
pastry	点心
pancake	煎饼
appetizer	开胃小吃/头盘
salad	色拉
dessert	甜点
rare	三分熟
medium	五分熟
well-done	全熟
caviar	鱼子酱
goose liver	鹅肝

Ⅱ. Pronunciation 语音训练

1. Are you ready to order, sir? / May I take your order, sir?
   先生，准备好点菜了吗？
2. What would you like to have, coffee or tea?
   您要喝咖啡还是茶？
3. Would you like an aperitif?
   您要不要来点开胃酒？
4. Would you care for a drink with your dinner?
   您在餐间要不要来点酒？
5. What would you like for your main course?
   主菜您点什么？
6. How would you like your steak to be done?
   您的牛排要几分熟？
7. What would you like to go with your steak?
   牛排的配菜要点什么？
8. I'm sorry, we have run out of it. But we have…
   很抱歉，这个菜今天卖完了，但是我们有……
9. Today's special is seafood.
   今天的特色菜是海鲜。
10. It's our chef's recommendation.
    这是我们主厨的推荐菜。
11. Do you prefer a la carte or table d'hote?
    您喜欢零点还是套餐？
12. What would you like for your dessert?
    甜点来点什么呢？
13. You may sign the bill. The hotel will charge you when you leave.
    您可以签单。离店时会给您结账。
14. I'm sorry, but I didn't quite catch what you just said.
    对不起，我没有听明白您刚才的话。
15. I beg your pardon? /Pardon?
    对不起，请再说一遍。
16. Sorry, sir, but I don't understand what you mean.
    很抱歉，先生，我没有听懂您的意思。
17. Pardon, madam. I am afraid I didn't follow you.
    对不起，女士，我没有听明白。
18. How would you like the steak/eggs?

您喜欢怎么样做的牛排/鸡蛋？

19. May I suggest California red wine for the steak?

    我建议您喝加利福尼亚红酒配牛排。

20. We look forward to having you soon.

    我们期待您下次光临。

Section B

Serivce Procedure 服务流程

1. Receive diners.
   迎客。
2. Seat the guest.
   安排入座。
3. Offer iced water and menu.
   上冰水和菜单。
4. Take the order.
   点菜。
5. Serve the dishes.
   上菜。
6. Take the bill.
   结账。
7. Bid farewell to the guest.
   送客。

Ⅰ. Service Performance 服务演练

W＝Waitress（服务生）　　G1＝Guest 1（客人甲）　　G2＝Guest 2（客人乙）

W：Good evening. Welcome to our restaurant. Have you made a reservation?

晚上好，欢迎光临。请问有预订吗？

G1：No, we haven't.

没有预订。

W：Only two of you?

是两位吗？

G2：Yes.

是的。

W：This way, please. How about this table?
这边请。这张餐台怎么样?

G1：It's fine.
很好。

W：Are you ready to order now, madam?
女士,可以点餐了吗?

G1：For an appetizer, I'll have smoked salmon. John, what would you like to have?
来一道开胃菜——熏三文鱼。约翰,你要什么?

G2：I'll have the flatfish, please.
我要一份比目鱼。

W：And for the main course?
请问要什么主菜?

G1：Well, I would like some meat. Two T-bone steak, please.
我想来点肉,两份T骨牛排。

W：How would you like your steak done, madam?
牛排要几分熟?

G1：One well-done, the other medium.
一份全熟,另一份五分熟。

W：Would you like some vegetables, sir?
先生,需要来点蔬菜吗?

G2：I'll have some fresh peas.
我要新鲜的豌豆。

W：And you, madam, which salad would you like?
女士,您要什么样的色拉?

G1：I would like some fruit salad, please.
我要水果色拉。

W：OK! Which soup would you like, sir?
好的! 先生,你们要什么汤?

G2：Fish soup, French style.
法式鱼汤。

W：Certainly, sir. Anything for dessert, sir?
好的,先生。需要甜点吗?

G2：Strawberry ice cream for both, please.
两份草莓味冰激凌。

W: And will you have some drinks?
　　喝点什么吗？

G2: Some red wine, please.
　　红葡萄酒吧。

W: Anything else, madam?
　　还需要别的吗？

G1: No, thanks. Bring me the bill, please.
　　没有了，谢谢。结账吧。

W: Here it is, madam. The total is 968 yuan.
　　给您，女士，总共968元。

G1: Is the service charge included?
　　服务费算在内了吗？

W: Yes, madam, 10% service charge. Who would like to pay please?
　　算在内了，女士，10%的服务费。请问谁买单？

G1: It's me. Here is 1000 yuan.
　　我来，这是1000元。

W: Thank you. Here is the change, please check.
　　谢谢，这是找您的钱，请核对。

G1: Thank you for your good service.
　　谢谢你的服务。

W: We look forward to seeing you again.
　　我们期待您再次光临。

Ⅱ. Position Practice 岗位实训

★ Procedure of Western Food.（西餐程序）
　　appetizer 头盘
　　soup 羹汤
　　side order 副菜
　　main course 主菜
　　salad 色拉
　　dessert 甜食
　　coffee or tea 咖啡或茶

★ Famous Brands of Western Wines.（著名洋酒品牌）
　　Rémy Martin 人头马
　　Martell 马爹利

Gordon's Gin 哥顿金酒
Smirnoff 皇冠伏特加
Matini 马天尼
Cointreau 君度
Hennessy 轩尼诗
Black Label 黑方
Red Label 红方
Bols 波尔斯
Tequila 龙舌兰
Beefeater 必富达
Myers's Rum 美雅士朗姆酒

★ Menu（菜单）
carrot salad 胡萝卜色拉
vegetable salad 蔬菜色拉
mixed salad 什锦色拉
fruit salad 水果色拉
smoked salmon 熏三文鱼
braised goose liver in red wine 红酒鹅肝
pan-fried whole flatfish 煎比目鱼
mixed vegetables 什锦蔬菜
stuffed tomato 酿西红柿
sour mushrooms 酸蘑菇
fried fish with tomato sauce 番茄汁炸鱼
smoked herring 熏鲱鱼
sour cucumbers/pickled cucumbers 酸黄瓜
pickled cabbage 泡菜
rump steak 牛腿扒
T-bone steak T 骨牛排
beef steak with curry 咖喱牛排
roast veal 烤小牛肉
sautéd pork chop 嫩煎猪排
roast lamb 烤羔羊肉
ham and sausage 火腿香肠
abalone 鲍鱼
shark fin 鱼翅
scallops 干贝

lobster 龙虾
fried rice with sea food 海鲜炒饭
fried rice with beef 牛肉炒饭
mixed fried rice 什锦炒饭
Japanese udon 日式乌冬面
Borscht soup 罗宋汤

★ Table d'hote and a la carte.（套餐和零点）

1. Table d'hote means the restaurant menu offers 3 or more courses for one price：usually consisting of appetizer，two or three choices of main course and dessert. Beverages are not usually included.
   套餐是餐厅菜单中以设定的价格提供三道或者三道以上的菜肴，通常包括开胃小吃，两三种可供选择的主食和甜点。酒水一般不包含在内。

2. A la carte means that a guest orders his items individually according to the menu and each item has its own separate charge on the bill.
   零点是指客人根据菜单一道一道点菜，每一道菜的价格都是分开的。

Ⅲ. Listening Practice 听力实训

★ A. Listen to the recording，decide what each short dialogue is about and mark "√" where appropriate.

	Starter	Soup	Main Dish	Dessert	Drink
Dialogue 1					
Dialogue 2					
Dialogue 3					
Dialogue 4					
Dialogue 5					

★ B. Complete the following conversation.

Receptionist：Good evening，madam. _____?
Guest：Yes，for two people _____ of Clarkson.
Receptionist：Thank you，madam. This way，please.
...
Waiter：_____, madam?
Guest：Yes，I think so. I will have sole to begin with. Is it good?
Waiter：Oh，Yes，madam. _____.

Guest: Well, I'm going to have meat, T-bone steak, please.
Waiter: _____, madam?
Guest: Well-done please.
Waiter: _____?
Guest: Fresh peas with my sole.
Waiter: _____ something to drink with your meal?
Guest: Half a bottle of _____ will be all right.
Waiter: Certainly, madam.

Important 特别关注

▲ In general, a lady will not take orders directly and a gentleman will order it for her.
一般来说,男士为女士点餐,女士不直接点餐。

▲ It is not very normal for one person to order for the whole table. Each person orders separately, except in especially expensive restaurants.
一个人不适合点一桌人的菜,除非是在特别昂贵的餐厅,否则每个人应该各点各的菜。

Section C

Case and Development 案例与创新

Case 案例

Mrs. Brown enters the western restaurant for dinner. She can not decide between beef and tuna fish, and you recommend a tuna fish, the chef's specialty to her. She asks for wine and you suggest a white Bordeaux wine (法国波尔多地区产的白葡萄酒). She also takes a vanilla ice-cream. She doesn't want anything else before dinner. Everything is good.

Development 创新

- If a guest orders something that has already sold out, what should you do?
- What would a waiter do if the dishes the guests order can not be served immediately?
- What kind of guest can sign the bill in the restaurant?

技能实训 19　早餐服务 Breakfast Service

听力音频

Section A

Basic Knowledge for Position 岗位基础知识

Ⅰ. Word Stock 词库

breakfast menu	早餐餐牌；早餐菜单
American breakfast	美式早餐
continental breakfast	欧洲大陆式早餐
full English breakfast	全英式早餐
buffet breakfast	自助式早餐
Chinese breakfast	中式早餐
jam	果酱
butter	黄油
cream	奶油
oatmeal	麦片
oatmeal porridge	麦片粥
omelet	炒蛋卷
scrambled egg	炒蛋
boiled egg	煮蛋
fried egg	煎蛋
sunny side up	单面煎的
over easy	双面煎的
poached egg	温泉蛋，水煮嫩蛋
cookie	曲奇饼
toast	吐司；烤面包片
roll	面包卷
ham/bacon/sausage	火腿/培根/香肠
rice congee	白米粥
steamed buns	包子
steamed bread	馒头
noodles	面条

soya milk	豆浆
pickled vegetable	酱菜
sesame ball	芝麻球

🔊 Ⅱ. **Pronunciation** 语音训练

1. Would you like tea or coffee this morning?
   今天早上您是要喝茶还是喝咖啡？
2. How would you like your eggs?
   请问鸡蛋要怎么做？
3. The price includes bed and continental breakfast.
   这个价钱包括房费和一份欧洲大陆式早餐。
4. We have continental breakfast and full English breakfast.
   我们有欧洲大陆式早餐和全英式早餐。
5. May I have your meal voucher, please?
   请把餐券给我好吗？
6. Would you please show me your room card?
   请出示您的房卡好吗？
7. Sorry to have kept you waiting.
   抱歉让您久等了。
8. What kind of jam would you like?
   您要哪种果酱？
9. Would you like separate bills? / Would you like to go Dutch?
   账单分开吗？/餐费平摊吗？
10. Buffet breakfast is included in the room charge.
    房价已经包含了自助早餐。

Section B

Serivce Procedure 服务流程

1. Greetings.
   问候。
2. Make sure the number of diners and show the way.
   了解就餐人数，将宾客带到适当的餐桌。

3. Seat the guest.
   安排客人就座。
4. Make sure of the juice the guest would like to have. If no juice is wanted, offer the guest ice water.
   问清宾客需要何种果汁，如不需要则替宾客倒冰水。
5. Offer the guest menu.
   递呈菜单。
6. Take orders and pay special attention to boiled eggs, fried eggs and meat.
   点单，特别关注煮蛋、煎蛋还有肉类。
7. Serve the breakfast.
   上早餐。
8. Bid farewell to the guest.
   道别。

Ⅰ. Service Performance 服务演练

G= Guest（客人）　　　　W=Waitress（服务生）

W：Good morning, sir. Welcome to our restaurant.
　　早上好，先生，欢迎光临。
G：Thank you.
　　谢谢。
W：How many of you, please, sir?
　　先生，请问一共几位？
G：Just two. My wife is coming soon.
　　就两位，我的妻子很快就到。
W：Yes, sir. This way, please. How do you like this table?
　　好的，先生，请这边走。这张桌子可以吗？
G：Fine.
　　行。
W：Here's the menu, sir. May I take your order now?
　　先生，这是菜单。现在可以点单吗？
G：Yes, is there a price difference between continental breakfast and American breakfast?
　　可以，欧洲大陆式早餐和美式早餐的价格有何区别？
W：Yes, a continental breakfast is 88 yuan per person while an American breakfast is 158 yuan per person.
　　欧洲大陆式早餐每位88元，美式早餐每位158元。
G：Well, American breakfast for both of us.
　　好的。我们两人都要美式早餐。

W：Certainly, sir. Coffee or tea?
好的，先生，喝咖啡还是喝茶？

G：Two cups of coffee.
两杯咖啡。

W：What kind of juice would you like to have?
您要哪种果汁？

G：Tomato juice for me and pineapple juice for my wife.
我要番茄汁，我的妻子要菠萝汁。

W：Yes, sir. One tomato juice and one pineapple juice. For bread, would you like soft roll, toast or croissant?
好的，先生。一杯番茄汁，一杯菠萝汁。面包呢？您要早餐包、吐司还是牛角包？

G：Both my wife and I would take toast. And two oatmeal porridge.
我们两位都要吐司，还要两份燕麦粥。

W：Yes, sir, two toast, two oatmeal porridge. How about eggs?
好的，先生。两份吐司，两份燕麦粥。鸡蛋呢？

G：My wife likes a boiled egg, hard boiled and I want fried eggs, sunny side up.
我的妻子要水煮蛋，煮得老一点。我要煎蛋，单面煎。

W：Served with bacon, ham or sausage?
是配培根、火腿还是香肠？

G：With bacon, please.
培根吧。

W：Yes, sir. I'll bring them to you right away.
好的，先生。很快就可以给您拿来。

Ⅱ. Position Practice 岗位实训

★ Differences among three kinds of western breakfast. （三种西式早餐的不同）

Western breakfast can be divided into American breakfast, continental breakfast and full English breakfast. American breakfast usually consists of the following: chilled orange, eggs and bacon, ham or sausages, rolls or toast with butter and coffee or tea. Continental breakfast is basically the same as American breakfast except that eggs with bacon, ham or sausages are not served. It is light and simple. A Full English Breakfast may have black pudding, baked beans and fried bread and eggs but may not include meat.

西式早餐可分为美式、欧洲大陆式和全英式三种。美式早餐通常包含冰果汁、新鲜的蛋和培根（或者火腿、香肠）、黄油吐司、咖啡或茶。欧洲大陆式早餐量小简单，一般无蛋无肉，其他的食物与美式早餐差不多。全英式早餐可能会提供黑布丁、烤豌豆、烤面包和鸡蛋，但没有肉。

★ Make sure how the guest would like his eggs.（确认客人要什么样的鸡蛋）
How do you like your eggs? Fried, poached, boiled or scrambled?
您想怎么做鸡蛋？煎蛋、荷包蛋、煮蛋，还是炒蛋？
★ Make sure how the guest would like his fried eggs.（确认客人要什么样的煎蛋）
How do you like your fried eggs? Sunny side up or over easy?
您要鸡蛋怎么煎？单面煎还是双面煎？
★ Make sure how the guest would like his boiled eggs.（确认客人要什么样的煮蛋）
How do you like your boiled eggs? Soft boiled or hard boiled?
您要鸡蛋怎么煮？煮得嫩一点还是老一点？

Ⅲ. Listening Practice 听力实训

★ A. Listen to the short passage and note the difference of American breakfast and continental breakfast.

Difference	Description	Place	Offer
American Breakfast			
Continental Breakfast			

★ B. Complete the following conversation.

Waiter: Good morning, sir.
Guest: Good morning. How are you this morning?
Waiter: I'm fine. Thank you, sir. _____?
Guest: Yes, I did. Thank you.
Waiter: _____?
Guest: Coffee, please. Make it really hot.
Waiter: All right, sir.
Guest: And I'll have some cornflakes, one fried egg and two pieces of toast, please.
Waiter: Cornflakes, one fried egg and two pieces of toast. And _____
_____?
Guest: Oh, over easy, please. Thank you.
Waiter: _____?
Guest: Bacon, please. And make it crispy, please.
Waiter: Just a minute, sir.
Guest: Thank you.
Waiter: _____.
Guest: That's all right, thank you.
Waiter: Would you like more coffee?

Guest: No. Thank you.

Important 特别关注

▲ More than 70% of the room service is breakfast.
早餐占客房送餐服务的 70% 以上。
▲ Whole-grain toast with a fresh juice, one cup of low-fat milk or yogurt is good for your breakfast.
全麦吐司配一杯鲜榨果汁,再加一杯低脂牛奶或酸奶作为早餐很不错。

Section C

Case and Development 案例与创新

Case 案例

Guest: You are from Sydney. You are having breakfast in a restaurant. You'd like to try a typical Chinese breakfast.

Waiter: Ask what the guest would like. Introduce some typical Chinese dim sum to the guest.

Development 创新

- What are the differences between a continental breakfast and a full English one?
- If breakfast is not served timely, how can you deal with the guests' complaint?
- How would you introduce the typical Chinese breakfast to a foreigner?

实训模块四 餐饮服务 Food and Beverage

技能实训 20　酒吧服务 At the Bar

听力音频

Section A

Basic Knowledge for Position 岗位基础知识

I . Word Stock 词库

bartender	调酒师
barman	酒吧男招待
barmaid	酒吧女招待
recipe	食谱；配方
champagne	香槟酒
cocktail	鸡尾酒
apple cider	苹果酒
whiskey	威士忌
brandy	白兰地
vodka	伏特加
rum	朗姆酒
gin	杜松子酒/金酒/琴酒
bitters	苦精
liquor	烈性酒；含酒精饮料
spirits	烈酒；烈性酒
draught beer	生啤
still wine	无气泡的酒
sparkling wine	有气泡的酒
distilled wine	蒸馏酒
fortified wine	加度葡萄酒
red wine	红葡萄酒
white wine	白葡萄酒
dry red wine	干红
base wine	基酒
chaser	追饮酒（饮淡酒后喝的烈性酒或饮烈性酒后喝的淡酒）
night cap	夜酒，睡前酒

straight up	纯饮
on the rocks	加冰
proof	标准酒精度（美国较常使用的酒精计量单位，是酒精度数的一半）
sober up	醒酒
tie me up	续杯
age	陈年
cellar	酒窖
close the bar	收吧

Ⅱ. Pronunciation 语音训练

1. What can I get for you, sir?
   先生，给您来点什么？
2. What would you like to drink?
   您要喝点什么？
3. Straight up or on the rocks?
   纯饮还是加冰？
4. With or without ice? /Up or down?
   加冰还是不加冰？
5. Tie me up, please.
   请再来一杯。
6. Do you like to have a drink with us?
   你要不要和我们去喝一杯啊？
7. I'll buy you a drink.
   我请你喝一杯吧。
8. It's on me. /My treat.
   我请客。
9. Draught beer, please.
   请给我生啤酒。
10. Do you want domestic or imported beer?
    你是要国产的还是进口的啤酒？
11. I am still sober.
    我还很清醒。
12. If you want to puke, just go ahead.
    如果你想吐的话，就去吧。
13. Cheers! /Bottoms up. /Let's make a toast.

干杯!

14. Would you like to have cocktail or whisky on the rocks?
    您要鸡尾酒还是要威士忌加冰?

15. Please bring me a pot of hot coffee.
    请给我一壶热咖啡。

16. There is a floor show in our lobby bar. Would you like to see it?
    大堂酒吧里有表演,您愿意去看吗?

17. Please feel free to tell us if you have any request.
    请尽管把您的要求告诉我们。

18. Miss Chen is regarded as one of the best barmaids in the bar.
    陈小姐被认为是酒吧里最好的女调酒师。

19. Here is the wine list, sir. Please take your time.
    先生,这是酒单,请慢慢看。

20. I do apologize. Is there anything I can do for you?
    非常抱歉,还有什么可以为您效劳吗?

21. The base of old fashioned cocktail is whiskey.
    古典鸡尾酒的基酒是威士忌。

22. Honestly speaking, I don't like this wine.
    老实说,我不喜欢这种酒。

Section B

Serivce Procedure 服务流程

1. Greetings.
   问候。

2. Seat the guest.
   领座。

3. Take orders for the guest.
   为客人点酒。

4. Prepare the wine for the guest.
   为客人调酒。

5. Serve the wine to the guest.
   为客人上酒。

6. Settle the account.
   为客人结账。

7. Bid farewell to the guest.
   道别。

🔊 Ⅰ. Service Performance 服务演练

G1＝Guest 1（客人甲）　　G2＝Guest 2（客人乙）　　W＝Waitress（服务生）

W：Anything to drink, gentlemen?
喝点什么吗，先生们？

G1：Well, we've been drinking whisky a lot. We'd like to have a change. Can you recommend some famous Chinese liquors?
哦，我们经常喝威士忌，今天想换换口味。你能向我们介绍一些中国酒吗？

W：What about Wuliangye, one of the most famous liquors in China? It's made from five kinds of cereal grains. It's fragrant and it never goes to the head.
五粮液怎么样？它是中国的名酒之一，由五谷酿制而成，非常芳香，而且不上头。

G1：All right, we'll have some.
好吧，来点五粮液。

W：May I remind you all the Chinese liquors are served by the bottle here?
提醒您一下，中国酒都是按瓶卖的。

G1：I see. Any other brands of liquor?
我明白，还有其他的品牌吗？

W：Yes, Maotai, Fenjiu, Swellfun, etc.
有的，还有茅台、汾酒、水井坊，等等。

G2：I hear Great Wall wine is a famous brand.
我听说长城葡萄酒是著名品牌。

W：Yes, it is. Would you like to try one bottle?
是的。您是否要来一瓶？

G2：OK, bring me the white wine as well. Make sure it is well chilled.
好的，我要白葡萄酒。记住要冰镇的。

W：Yes, sir. A bottle of well chilled white wine. Have you ever heard about Shaoxing wine? It's a kind of still wine made from rice, somewhat like Japanese sake.
好的，先生。一瓶冰镇白葡萄酒。你们有没有听说过绍兴黄酒？它是一种用米酿制的酒，有点像日本的清酒。

G1：I have, but you see we've got enough, we'll have a drink next time.
我听说过，但我们今天点得够多了，下次再喝吧。

W: Yes, sir. So you've ordered one bottle of Wuliangye and one bottle of Great Wall white wine. Just a moment, please, gentlemen.

好的，先生。你们点的是一瓶五粮液、一瓶长城白葡萄酒。请稍等，先生们。

Ⅱ. Position Practice 岗位实训

★ Classification of bars. （酒吧的分类）

Lobby Bar 大堂吧

Lobby Lounge 大堂酒廊

Main Bar 主酒吧（装饰考究、别致，客人可以全面欣赏调酒师的全套操作过程）

Cash Bar （婚礼、聚会等场合的）售饮料柜台

Service Bar 服务酒吧（与主酒吧相比相对简单，调酒师不需要直接与客人打交道）

Theme Bar 主题酒吧（特点突出，以销售饮料为主）

Grand Bar 多功能酒吧（大多设在娱乐场所）

Banquet Bar 宴会酒吧（临时为宴会设立的酒吧，供应酒水的品种比较随意）

★ Introduce different kinds of drinks to the guest. （向客人介绍不同的饮料）

soft drink 不含酒精的饮料

hard drink 含酒精的饮料

cold drink 冷饮

mineral water 矿泉水

green tea 绿茶

black tea 红茶

black coffee 清咖啡

white coffee 奶咖啡

soda water 苏打水

★ Introduce cocktail decorations to the guest. （向客人介绍鸡尾酒上的装饰）

cherry 樱桃

lemon 柠檬

clove 丁香

pineapple 菠萝

onion 洋葱

strawberry 草莓

olive 橄榄

cucumber 黄瓜

mint 薄荷

grapefruit 西柚

★ Be familiar with bar tools. (熟悉酒吧用具)
counter 吧台
stool 高脚凳
bottle opener 开瓶刀
corkscrew 螺旋形开瓶器
ice shaver 削冰器，冰刨
ice maker 制冰机
ice bucket 小冰桶
cocktail shaker 调酒器
pouring measure 量酒器
electric blender 电动搅拌机
straw 吸管
bar spoon 调酒匙

★ Get to know famous foreign wines. (了解外国名酒)

威士忌（whiskey）：威士忌是一种烈性蒸馏酒，主要分为苏格兰威士忌（Scotch Whiskey）、爱尔兰威士忌（Irish Whiskey）、加拿大威士忌（Canadian Whiskey）和美国威士忌（American Whiskey）。

金酒（gin）：金酒也称杜松子酒或琴酒，可分为荷兰式金酒和英国式金酒两类。荷兰式金酒色泽透明清亮，香味突出，风格独特，适宜单饮。英国金酒也称为干金酒，酒液无色透明，气味奇异清香，口感醇美爽适。

伏特加（vodka）：伏特加是俄罗斯最具有代表性的白酒，无色且清淡爽口，无须贮存即可出售。伏特加与金酒一样无色透明，可与其他酒类混合调成各种混合饮品和鸡尾酒。

白兰地（brandy）：白兰地是一种蒸馏酒，以水果为原料，经过发酵、蒸馏、贮藏后酿造而成。法国是世界上首屈一指的白兰地生产国。法国人引以为豪的白兰地叫干邑（Cognac），是世界上同类产品中最受欢迎的一种，有"白兰地之王"的美誉。

香槟（champagne）：香槟是指产于法国香槟区的符合一系列特殊标准的葡萄酒。香槟在开瓶后，会爆出巨响，冒出泡沫，经常用于增添喜庆气氛。

苦艾酒（vermouth）：苦艾酒芳香浓郁，口感清淡且略带苦味，一般都当作餐前酒，也经常用来调制鸡尾酒。

朗姆酒（rum）：朗姆酒是以甘蔗糖蜜为原料生产的一种蒸馏酒，原产地在古巴。朗姆酒按颜色也可分为三类，即白朗姆酒（Silver Rum）、金朗姆酒（Golden Rum）和黑朗姆酒（Dark Rum）。

鸡尾酒（cocktail）：鸡尾酒通常以朗姆酒、金酒、伏特加、威士忌、白兰地等烈酒或葡萄酒作为基酒，再加上果汁、蛋清、苦精、牛奶、糖等调制而成，常用于各种宴会。

Ⅲ. Listening Practice 听力实训

★ A. Listen to the recording, decide what each short is about and mark "√" where appropriate.

	Liquor	Cocktail	Soft Drink	Wine	Traditional Drink
Dialogue 1					
Dialogue 2					
Dialogue 3					
Dialogue 4					
Dialogue 5					

★ B. A waiter is introducing some kinds of wines to the guest. Try to fill in the missing information.

1. Bordeaux is a _____ from southwest France.
2. Rioja is a full-bodied red wine _____.
3. Chablis is a very dry white wine _____.
4. Chianti is _____ from Italy.
5. You may like an Australian Chardonnay, which _____ your lobster.
6. Bourbon whiskey is a type of _____ whiskey—a distilled spirit _____.
7. Burgundy wine is made in the Burgundy region in _____.
8. Sauternes is a _____ wine.

Important 特别关注

▲ Barstool positions are often numbered for the bar staff and food runners. Never move barstools without permission.
为方便酒吧员工送餐，吧椅通常都有编号。没有得到许可不得移动吧椅。

▲ Introduce yourself and learn your bartender's name. Using a bartender's name makes the interaction more respectful and humanized. But never shout the bartender's name loudly to get his attention.
自我介绍并记住酒吧侍者的名字，用名字称呼酒吧侍者使得沟通更显尊敬和人性化，但是千万不能为了引起他的关注而大喊他的名字。

▲ Never ask dreadful and insulting questions, for example, is this your real job? Or,

What else do you do?

永远不要问愚蠢的带有侮辱性的问题，比如：这是你真正的工作吗？或者你还做其他什么工作？

▲ Sharing your personal issues (especially quarrels between couples) with the rest of the bar makes everyone uncomfortable. Remember that you're sharing space with other people. Control your volume.

你个人的问题（尤其是夫妻之间的吵架）拿来跟其他人讨论会让别人感到不舒服。记住你跟别人共享同一个空间，注意控制你的声音。

Section C

Case and Development 案例与创新

Case 案例

Bartender：You greet the guest and ask him of his order. You make a few suggestions on Chinese liquors. You take the order and serve the drink.

Guest：You ask for a typical Chinese drink. You take one of the recommendations. And you ask the business hours of the bar. You accept the advice given by the bartender and pay your bill.

Development 创新

- What qualifications should a bartender have?
- What can you do if you notice a guest has drunk too much?
- Make a presentation of mixing cocktail.

技能实训 21　就餐礼仪 Table Manners

听力音频

Section A

Basic Knowledge for Position 岗位基础知识

I. Word Stock 词库

table manners	餐桌礼仪
custom	习俗
etiquette	礼仪
difference	不同点
similarity	相同点
compare	比较
appropriate	合适的
utensil	器皿
culture	文化
observe	遵守
standard	标准
elegant	优雅的
acceptable	可以接受的
offensive	冒犯的
appetite	胃口
edible	可以食用的
knife and fork	刀叉
napkin	餐巾
table cloth	桌布
tableware	餐具
salad fork	沙拉餐叉
dinner fork	正餐叉
steak knife	牛排刀
butter knife	黄油刀
soup spoon	汤勺
tea spoon	茶匙

Ⅱ. Pronunciation 语音训练

1. Would you like to have some wine with your dinner?
   您用餐时要喝点酒吗?
2. What would you like to drink, beer, champagne, wine or Maotai?
   你们想喝点什么? 啤酒、香槟、葡萄酒还是茅台?
3. Have you decided what to drink?
   您决定喝什么了吗?
4. What kind of food would you like to have?
   您想吃什么菜?
5. What kind of sauce would you like?
   您要加哪种酱汁?
6. It's delicious and worth a try.
   它鲜美可口,值得一试。
7. I do apologize for giving you the wrong soup.
   我上错了汤,真抱歉。
8. Sorry for that, may I help you heat it?
   很抱歉,帮你加热一下好吗?

Section B

Table Manners 就餐礼仪

Seat the guest 入座

You should take your seat from the left unless the left is against the wall. Gentleman or host is supposed to sit by the aisle so that ladies or guests can sit against the wall. Napkins by your left hand and glasses by your right hand are for you.

要从座位的左侧入座,除非左侧靠墙。男士或者主人应该坐在靠过道的位置,让女士或者客人坐在靠墙的位置。左侧的纸巾和右侧的杯子是自己使用的。

★ Bread before dinner. (餐前小面包)

Bread is taken with fingers, it is never taken with a fork. Even bread is very small, you should tear it by pieces and have it piece by piece.

用手指拿着面包,绝对不要用叉子吃面包。即使面包很小,也一定要一小块一小块地撕下来塞进嘴里。

★ The soup course.（汤）

Dinner usually begins with soup. The largest spoon at your place is the soup spoon. It will be beside your plate by the right hand. Use your spoon to drink soup and don't take too much soup at a time in case it may spread and it's impolite as well. Never utter noises or blow it when having soup. Remember to keep quiet always!

正餐通常从汤开始。你的位置上最大的那把勺子就是汤匙，放在你餐盘的右手边。汤要用汤匙慢慢舀起来送到嘴巴里，舀的时候不要装太多，那样看起来很没有礼貌，同时也可以避免中途汤汁滴落。喝汤时切忌发出响声或吹气。记得吃西餐时始终要保持安静。

★ The fish course.（鱼）

If there is a fish course, it will probably follow the soup. There may be a special fork for the fish. Often it is smaller than the meat fork.

如果正餐中有鱼的话，一般就在汤后面。有可能会提供专门的鱼叉，鱼叉通常要比肉叉小一点。

★ The meat course.（肉）

The majority of meat courses (with the exception of poultry and ham) will be served with red wines. Generally, simply cooked roasts need better bottles and those with more age. Spicy dishes or those with lots of different flavours would be better with younger wines. When you cut a piece of steak, you should have it right now. Never cut the steak into pieces at one time, cold steak won't be so delicious.

吃绝大部分的肉时（除了家禽和火腿）都会配红酒。一般来说，简单烧烤的肉需要好一点的、年份久一点的红酒，而一些有辣味或添加了许多调味品的肉就选用清淡一点的红酒。吃牛排时应该切一块吃一块。不要一次把肉全都切开，牛排冷了就不好吃了。

★ The salad course.（色拉）

A salad is eaten with a fork only held in the right hand with points turned up.

吃色拉时只能用叉子，右手持叉，叉子的尖朝上。

★ Dessert and beverage.（甜点和饮料）

If there are some decorations in the dessert that are not edible, the waiter will tell you in advance, or you should eat them up. The last course is coffee or tea. The small tea spoon is to stir sugar and coffee mate, it is not used to drink coffee. You should hold coffee cup and drink it slowly.

如果甜点上有不可食用的缀饰，服务生会明确告诉你，否则还是要把甜点全部吃完。最后会上咖啡或茶，调羹是用来搅拌糖和咖啡伴侣的，不是用来舀咖啡喝的。喝的时候用手端起杯子慢慢喝。

I. Position Practice 岗位实训

★ What does 6M represent in a Western restaurant?（西餐厅中的6M代表什么？）

1. Menu: In a restaurant, a menu is a printed brochure that shows the list of options for a diner to select.
   菜单：在餐厅中，菜单是指为就餐者提供的列有各种菜肴选择的清单。
2. Music: Deluxe Western restaurants should have a band and play soft music.
   音乐：豪华的西餐厅要有乐队，演奏一些柔和的乐曲。
3. Mood: Surround the dining area with scented candles, dim the lights, and scatter rose petals on the table. Keep it tasteful, and harmonious.
   气氛：就餐的地方如果点有香薰蜡烛，灯光暗淡，餐桌上撒有玫瑰花瓣，会显得非常有品位和和谐。
4. Meeting: The world is full of romantic places where you can spend time of high quality. A Western restaurant is really a good choice.
   会面：世界上有许多浪漫的地方可以让你度过高品质的时光，西餐厅绝对是好选择。
5. Manner: Table manners are the rules of etiquette that we should observe while eating. Different cultures observe different rules of table manners. Pay attention to what you should do and what you shouldn't do.
   礼仪：餐桌礼仪是用餐的时候要遵循的规则。不同的文化有不同的餐桌礼仪。注意你该做什么、不该做什么。
6. Meal: Western food is simple while Chinese food is relatively complicated, and more delicious.
   食品：西餐的食物比较简单，而中餐的食物相对比较复杂，也更美味。

★ Using knife and fork. （刀叉的使用）

If you have English and American friends, you will notice a few differences in using knife and fork. For the main or meat course, the English hold the fork in the left hand, point curved downward, and bring the food to the mouth by sticking the points onto it. While Americans carve the meat first of all, then lay down the knife and hold the fork in the right hand, pick up a small piece of food with fork and bring it to the mouth.

如果你有美国和英国的朋友的话，你可能会发现他们使用刀叉的习惯略有不同。在上主菜或肉菜时，英国人用左手拿叉，叉头朝下，把食物叉上再送入口；而美国人则在切分好肉以后，把刀放下，换用右手拿叉，叉起一小块食物送入口中。

★ Helping yourself and refusing. （自助与拒绝）

When a waiter serves the dish, he will serve the dish in at your left hand so that you can conveniently serve yourself with your right hand. Never serve yourself while the dish is on your right, it is the dish of your neighbor on the right. It is polite to take some of the dishes that are served to you. But if there is something that you may not like, you may quietly say: "No, thank you."

如果服务生分菜，他会把菜放在你的左手边方便你用右手取菜。如果菜在你的右手边,这是你的邻座的菜,而不该你取菜。取一点向你递过来的菜是礼貌的做法。如果真的不喜欢这道菜,就轻轻地说一声:"不用了,谢谢。"

Ⅱ. Listening Practice 听力实训

★ A. Listen to the following passage about table manners and fill in the missing information.

Table manners are the _____ of etiquette used while eating. _____ observe different rules for table manners. Many people _____ when dining simply because they don't know how to follow _____, especially if they have been _____ a nice place. Talking about table manners, unlike the West where everyone has _____ of food, in China the dishes are placed on the table and everybody _____. If you are being treated by a Chinese host, be prepared for a ton of food. And sometimes the host will _____ with his or her own chopsticks to guests to show his or her hospitality. This is a sign of _____. If you feel _____ with this, you can just say a polite "thank you" and _____ there. There are some other rules that are suggested to you follow to make your stay in China happier, though you will be forgiven if you _____ what they are.

★ B. Listen to the statements and put a "DO" or a "DON'T" in front of each statement.

1. _____ eat and drink at the same time.
2. _____ chew with your mouth open.
3. _____ put elbows on the table.
4. _____ wipe your mouth with the corners of your napkin.
5. _____ sit up straight while eating.
6. _____ eat and talk at the same time.
7. _____ place your silverware on the table after use.
8. _____ place your napkin on your lap before eating.
9. _____ make loud eating noises.
10. _____ use a napkin to clean your face.
11. _____ excuse yourself if you must leave the table during a meal.
12. _____ stand up to get the salt if it is out of your reach.

Important 特别关注

▲ Sit up straight on your chair.
坐在椅子上要保持身体笔直。

▲ Don't eat with your hands.
不要用手拿东西吃。

▲ Do not put much food in your mouth at a time.
不要一次塞太多食物进嘴巴。

▲ Drink only when there is no food in your mouth.
只有当你的嘴巴没有食物的时候才喝酒水。

▲ Do not make any noise when you eat.
吃饭的时候不要发出噪声。

▲ Do not clean your teeth at the table or anywhere in public, either with your finger or a tooth pick, not even with your tongue.
不要在餐桌或其他公众场合清洁你的牙齿,不管是用手指还是牙签,哪怕是用舌头也不行。

▲ When passing someone an item such as the salt shaker, put it on the table in front of the person, not in his hand.
当传递比如盐罐之类的东西给某人的时候,应放在他的前面,而不是放在他的手里。

▲ Don't put your elbows on the table.
不要把胳膊肘搁在桌子上。

▲ Eat slowly and pace your eating to that of the others at the table.
慢慢吃,与餐桌上的其他人保持同步。

▲ When in doubt, do what the natives do. Watch and imitate.
如果有疑问,就按当地人的做法去做。观察并模仿他们。

Section C

Case and Development 案例与创新

Case 案例

Work with your partner and brainstorm a list of table manners. Then compare and contrast your list with lists of others. You are encouraged to talk about dinner table manners in your families and customs practiced in your homes. Each person can make a "Top Tens at My Table" poster to share with the class.

Development 创新

• Can you identify the similarities and differences between Chinese and American dinner table manners?

- Do you know any special table manners in other countries?
- What table manners do you think everyone should observe? What table manners do you think are not necessary in our culture?

实训模块五

康乐中心
Recreation Center

As an auxiliary part to a hotel, Recreation Center aims first of all to provide an excellent service for the guests. The service in Recreation Center has all the characteristics of other hotel services, for example, enthusiasm, politeness, patience and consideration etc. Besides, it has many unique features as well.

康乐中心的首要功能是作为酒店的配套附属设施,目标是为客人提供高质量的接待服务。康乐中心的服务与酒店的其他服务有许多共性,如热情好客、文明礼貌、耐心周到等。除此之外,它还有许多鲜明的特征。

听力音频

技能实训 22　健身服务 Gym Service

Section A

Basic Knowledge for Position 岗位基础知识

I. Word Stock 词库

gym/gymnasium	健身房，体操房
fitness center	健身中心
health club	健身俱乐部
get fit	保持体态
lose weight	减肥
gain weight	增重
build muscle	增强肌肉
shape your body	塑身
fitness coach	健身教练
sneaker	运动鞋
locker	置物柜
membership fee	入会费
ball games	球类运动
basketball	篮球
bowling	保龄球
volleyball	排球
badminton	羽毛球
golf	高尔夫球
tennis	网球
table tennis/ping-pong	乒乓球
basketball court	篮球场
go bowling	打保龄球
bowling alley	保龄球馆
golf course	高尔夫球场
indoor tennis court	室内网球场

outdoor tennis court	室外网球场
warm up	作准备活动
bodybuilding exercise	健美（身）运动
shape-up exercise	形体训练
bodybuilder	健美运动员
Miss World	世界小姐

Ⅱ. Pronunciation 语音训练

1. We have a well-equipped gym with the latest recreational sports apparatus.
   我们有设备良好的健身房，里面有最新式的娱乐体育器械。

2. It's becoming a trend for modern people to work out in the gym.
   现代人在健身房健身已成为一种趋势。

3. A calorie-controlled diet will help those who want to lose weight.
   对于减肥人士来说，控制热量的饮食会很有帮助。

4. I work out every day in order to build the muscle in my chest and arms and get rid of the fat around my waist.
   我每天健身是为了增加我胸部和手臂的肌肉，并消除腰部的脂肪。

5. We all should warm up before doing some exercises.
   开始做运动前，我们都应该做热身运动。

6. Every time you work out you should begin and end with a few stretches.
   每次健身的前后，我们都应该做一些伸展的动作。

7. You can use a heart rate monitor to know your heart rate.
   你可以使用心跳监测器得知你的心率。

8. Our body need a certain amount of time to metabolize fats.
   我们的身体需要足够的时间来把脂肪代谢掉。

9. Bowling is a kind of sports which has a long history and many people are keen on it.
   保龄球是一项历史悠久的体育项目，深受人们喜欢。

10. Hope you all have a pleasant time. If you need any help, please let me know at once.
    祝你们玩得愉快，有什么需要帮忙的尽管告诉我。

Section B

Service Procedure 服务流程

1. Greetings.
   问候。
2. Introduce service items and facilities.
   介绍服务项目和设施。
3. Introduce the charge.
   介绍费用。
4. Examine the room card.
   检查房卡。
5. Go through the procedure.
   办手续。
6. Lead the guest to the place.
   带客人到指定位置。
7. Settle the account.
   结账。
8. Bid farewell to the guest.
   道别。

Ⅰ. Service Performance 服务演练

A＝Attendant（服务生）　　　G＝Guest（客人）

A：Hello! Welcome to the table tennis room. I'm Liu Fang, an attendant here. It's my pleasure to serve you.
您好！欢迎光临乒乓球室！我是这里的服务生刘方，能为您服务不胜荣幸！

G：Hello! The room looks nice and bright.
你好！这里看起来很宽敞明亮。

A：Yes. You know table tennis is popular not only in China, but many countries in the world. We want to give our guests first-class practice here.
是的。您知道乒乓球不仅在中国很普及，在世界很多国家也很受欢迎。所以，我们希望能在这里给我们的客人提供一流的体验。

G：Wonderful! We are sure we'll enjoy ourselves here.
太好了！我们肯定会玩得很开心。

A：Do you like watching table tennis match? Can you name some of the Chinese famous table tennis players?

您喜欢看乒乓球比赛吗？您能说出一些中国著名的乒乓球选手的名字吗？

G：Sure, I do. Deng Yaping, Wang Nan for Women's, and Liu Guoliang, Ma Lin for Men's, they are famous all over the world.

当然知道。女子的有邓亚萍、王楠，男子的有刘国梁、马琳等，他们在全世界都是很著名的。

A：Great! How many people are there in your party?

真棒！请问你们一共有几位？

G：There are altogether five of us. Can we have two tables?

我们一共有五位。我们可以用两个乒乓球桌吗？

A：Certainly you can. We charge each table 100 RMB for an hour. Please remember to pay the bill in the service counter when you leave.

当然可以。每张球桌每小时收费100元人民币。请在活动结束后到服务台办理结账手续。

G：OK. That is acceptable. We want two.

好的，这个价格可以接受。我们要两张球桌。

A：Do you have your own table tennis bat and ball? If you don't have, we can provide you free of charge.

你们有自己的乒乓球拍和乒乓球吗？如果你们没有，我们可以免费提供。

G：Thank you.

谢谢！

A：Anything you want to drink?

请问你们要喝点什么？

G：Just bottles of mineral water.

来几瓶矿泉水就可以了。

A：OK. Is there anything else I can do for you?

好的。请问还有其他需要吗？

G：Not now. Thank you!

现在没有了。谢谢！

A：Hope you all have a wonderful time. If you need any help, don't hesitate to let me know.

祝你们玩得愉快！有什么需要帮忙的请告诉我。

Ⅱ．Position Practice 岗位实训

★ What are included in gym service?（健身运动包括哪些项目？）

It mainly includes basketball, volleyball, badminton, tennis, golf, table tennis, bowling, arrow shooting, gymnastics, etc. Different hotels provide different service according to their own conditions.

它主要包括篮球、排球、羽毛球、网球、高尔夫球、乒乓球、保龄球、射箭、体操等健身项目。不同的酒店会根据自身情况设置不同的项目。

★ Grand Slam Tennis. （网球四大满贯）
Wimbledon Championships 温布尔登网球锦标赛
French Open 法国网球公开赛
U. S. Open 美国网球公开赛
Australian Open 澳大利亚网球公开赛

★ Introduce the gym service. （向客人介绍健身项目）
We offer many kinds of gym service, such as basketball, volleyball, table tennis, etc. You can also swim in the swimming pool.

我们有很多类型的健身服务，比如篮球、排球、乒乓球等。您还可以去游泳池游泳。

★ Introduce the price of each gym service. （向客人介绍各个健身项目的价格）
Can I introduce the rate for each kind of sports?
我能向您介绍各个运动项目的价格吗？

★ Remind guests of the matters that they shall pay attention to when doing sports. （提醒客人注意事项）

You'd better do some warm-up training before the exercises, in order to avoid ankle sprain, muscle injury or knee hurt and other accidents.

在运动之前，请您先做好热身，以免发生脚踝扭伤、肌肉拉伤、膝盖损伤等意外事故。

★ Announce guests of settling account. （告诉客人结账事宜）
Would you please pay the bill at the service center after the training?
请您在运动后去服务台结账，可以吗？

★ Remind guests of indemnity for damage. （提醒客人损坏赔偿事宜）
According to the hotel rules, if there is any damage of the equipment, you will have to make the compensation with full price.

按照酒店的规定，如果有器械损坏，您将照原价赔偿。

Ⅲ. Listening Practice 听力实训

★ A. Listen to the following passage about gym service and fill in the missing information.

Like other travelers, you hope for a _____ at any hotel. With services like gym facilities, visitors in Radison Plaza Hotel find it a _____ for both _____ . The hotel provides a variety of services all designed for _____ _____ in mind. You will also be given _____ on technique and exercise advice during the exercise. Gym service _____ all the guests staying in our hotel. Gym service is included in your _____. Come to our gym center and _____ energetic!

★ B. Complete the following conversation.

Attendant: Good afternoon, sir. May I help you?
Guest: Yes, please. Life has been easy and _____.
Attendant: I think the best way to _____ is to do some exercises.
Guest: What activities do you offer?
Attendant: We offer _____, running, cycling, muscle building and chest expanding.
Guest: Do you have a coach here to supervise the exercises?
Attendant: Yes, we have a resident coach here. _____.
Guest: And your service hour?
Attendant: _____.
Guest: Good. I'll try cycling first.

Important 特别关注

▲ Remind the guests of changing sport shoes.
提醒客人要换运动鞋。
▲ Remind the guests of proper training.
提醒客人适量运动。
▲ Closely watch the guests in case of any accident.
密切关注客人，以免发生意外。

Section C

Case and Development 案例与创新

Case 案例

Suppose you work in the Recreation Department. Now there comes a long-stay guest. Make a conversation between two of you. The attendant should greet the guest and introduce the service to the guest while the guest should ask questions to get the information he needs.

Development 创新

- How much do you know about Tai Chi? Why does Tai Chi become more and more popular among foreigners?
- What advice can you give the guest to keep fit?
- What kind of lifestyle can be considered as a healthy one?

技能实训 23　美容美发服务
Beauty & Hair Salon

听力音频

Section A

Basic Knowledge for Position 岗位基础知识

I. Word Stock 词库

facial cleanser	洗面奶
day cream	日霜
night cream	晚霜
eye cream	眼霜
cosmetic	化妆品
lipstick	口红
pressed powder	粉饼
make-up (n.) / make up (v.)	化妆
bridal make-up	新娘妆
evening make-up	晚妆
day make-up	日妆
beauty salon	美容院
beautician	美容师
anti-ager and wrinkle-proof	抗老防皱
essence	精华液
foundation	粉底
clear lotion	化妆水
mask	面膜
normal skin	中性皮肤
oily skin	油性皮肤
remover	卸妆用品
permanent wave	烫发
cut hair	剪发，理发
dye hair	染发
hair design	发型设计
massage	按摩

full service	全套服务
eyebrow pencil	眉笔
cosmetic bag	化妆包
hairstyle	发型
hair stylist	理发师

Ⅱ. Pronunciation 语音训练

1. I want my hair dyed.
   我想染发。

2. Your current hairstyle does not suit you that much.
   您现在的发型不太适合您。

3. Can I have my hair thinned out a bit?
   能把我的头发打薄一点吗？

4. We have separate locker rooms over there. You can use them free of charge.
   我们有独立的带锁的更衣室，您可以免费使用。

5. The beard fits your face just perfectly.
   这个胡子很配您的脸型。

6. Would you like a facial massage?
   您需要脸部按摩吗？

7. Your personality shines through the proper hairstyle.
   您的个性可以通过合适的发型显示出来。

8. Have you taken a look at any of the recent hairstyles lately?
   您最近有没有看到什么新的发型？

9. I think you would look cute with short hair.
   我认为您剪短发一定很好看。

10. Do you think that would look good? I'm worried it will make my hair look unnatural.
    你认为那样会好看吗？我担心那会使我的头发看起来不自然。

Section B

Service Procedure 服务流程

1. Greetings.
   问候。

2. Introduce service items and facilities.

介绍服务项目和设施。

3. Introduce the charge.

    介绍费用。

4. Lead the guest to the place.

    带客人到指定位置。

5. Settle the account.

    结账。

6. Bid farewell to the guest.

    道别。

🔊 Ⅰ. **Service Performance 服务演练**

H= Hair stylist（理发师）　　G=Guest（客人）

H：It's been a long time, Mrs. Lee.

　　李太太，很久没见了。

G：Yes. I was on vacation in Sanya with my husband.

　　是的。我和我丈夫刚从三亚度假回来。

H：When did you come back? Did you have a good time?

　　什么时候回来的？玩得好吗？

G：We came back the day before yesterday. I enjoyed myself there very much. The beach was beautiful. The sun was lovely, too. You should go there some day.

　　我们是前天回来的，在那儿玩得很开心。那里的阳光和沙滩都漂亮极了，以后你也应该去玩玩。

H：I will. How would you like your hair to be done today? The same style as usual?

　　我会去的。今天打算做什么发型啊？和平时的一样吗？

G：I have a wedding ceremony to attend tonight, and I'd like to have a change.

　　我今晚要参加一个婚宴，我想改变一下发型。

H：Here are some samples of hairstyles. What do you think about this one?

　　这里有一些发型的款式。这个怎样？

G：No, I don't like short hair... I like this one. The wave looks beautiful, and fits my age too.

　　不，我不喜欢短发……我喜欢这个，波浪形看起来很漂亮，也适合我的年龄。

H：Very well. You're not in a hurry, are you?

　　好的。您不着急吧？

G：No. You can take your time... Oh, I also want a manicure while I'm having the perm.

　　不急，你慢慢来。哦，烫头发的时候我还想顺便修一下指甲。

H：OK. The manicurist will be right here.

好的。美甲师马上就过来。

G：Thank you. How much will this cost?

谢谢。一共多少钱？

H：It's five hundred and twenty yuan in all.

总共 520 元。

Ⅱ. Position Practice 岗位实训

★ Introduce the price of each item. （向客人介绍各项目价格）

That'll cost you 600 yuan, madam.

女士，那个项目要花 600 元。

★ How would you like your haircut? （你要剪什么样的发型）

Madam, we have various models: hair bobbed, hair sweptback, shoulder-length hairstyle, hair done in a bun.

女士，我们这里可以做各种各样的发型，比如短发、后掠式发型、齐肩发，还可以把头发换成发髻。

★ Introduce the cosmetology items. （向客人介绍美容项目）

The services which we can provide are skin-whitening, wrinkle-proofing, moist-keeping, and so on.

我们有美白、防皱、保湿等项目。

★ Announce guests of settling account. （告诉客人结账事宜）

Would you please pay the fee at the service center after the service?

请您在做完后去服务台结账，可以吗？

Ⅲ. Listening Practice 听力实训

★ A. Listen to the following passage about beauty salon and fill in the missing information.

There are many different kinds of ＿＿＿＿＿＿＿＿ . The different types of salon services provide ＿＿＿＿＿＿＿＿ for the body from head to toe. ＿＿＿＿＿＿＿＿ are the most common. The style of service varies in ＿＿＿＿＿＿＿＿ hairdressing salons. Day Spa salons may also serve guests tea ＿＿＿＿＿＿＿＿ a light lunch. Services at a day spa often ＿＿＿＿＿＿＿＿ massage, facials and skin care treatments. Many different types of salons feature ＿＿＿＿＿＿＿＿ . Makeup services are ＿＿＿＿＿＿＿＿ at many kinds of salons. Traditionally, salon cosmetic services ＿＿＿＿＿＿＿＿ women only, but increasingly, men's makeup options are also available.

实训模块五 康乐中心 Recreation Center

★ B. Complete the following conversation.

Beautician: Hi. _____?

Customer: Yeah. I'd like to get my hair trimmed a little. Nothing fancy. Just a basic trim.

Beautician: Well, can we interest you _____?

Customer: Um... Nah, nah...

Beautician: We'll shampoo, cut, and design your hairstyle for an unbelievable low price of _____.

Customer: Well, I don't know. I don't have much time, and ...

Beautician: _____!

Customer: Well, okay. I'll have the complete service today, but as I said before, I just want to get my hair trimmed. _____. That's all. I mean, that's all.

Beautician: _____. You're in good hands. Okay, here we go.

Customer: Hey, can I have a mirror?

Beautician: Nothing to worry about, sir. Relax. I've just making some adjustments to the hair trimmer.

Customer: Oh, that really hurt! What are you doing anyway?

Beautician: Relax, sir, relax. _____.

Customer: Yeah, just wait till I get finished with you!

Beautician: Okay, now let's dry your hair, if you're not completely satisfied...

Customer: Satisfied? _____. I want to talk to the manager... now!

Beautician: I'm sorry, but he's on vacation, and he left it to me, so if you...

Important 特别关注

▲ Using the proper terms of cosmetology, body-caring, etc.
使用美容、美体等专业术语。

▲ Pay attention to the complaints in cosmetology and body-caring, etc. and find solutions to them.
注意解决美容、美体等服务中的投诉。

▲ Remind the guests to ask to stop service in case of allergy.
提醒客人如有过敏症状,应及时停止。

Section C

Case and Development 案例与创新

Case 案例

The middle-aged lady is an American who teaches English at a university in Beijing. She wants to have a cold wave. You, the hairdresser, is serving her.

Development 创新

• How can you politely suggest a new hairstyle to the guest?

• If a guest's skin is very sensitive, what should be avoided when you do the facial massage?

• Why can a beautiful haircut make a person look more elegant?

技能实训 24　桑拿服务 Sauna Service

听力音频

Section A

Basic Knowledge for Position 岗位基础知识

I. Word Stock 词库

bathrobe	浴衣
celsius	摄氏的（adj.）/摄氏度（n.）
comfortable	舒适的
Fahrenheit	华氏的（adj.）/华氏度（n.）
festive	节日的，喜庆的
Finnish sauna	芬兰浴
fortune	财富，运气
inexperienced	没经验的，没经历过的
ingredient	成分，因素
inhabitant	居民，居住者
locker	橱柜，存物柜
shower gel	沐浴液
mental	精神的，智力的，脑力的
moisture	潮湿，湿气
relax	放松
sauna room	桑拿浴室
shower	淋浴
solely	独自地，单独地
stand	忍受
task	任务
temperature	温度

II. Pronunciation 语音训练

1. Welcome to our bathing center! What can I do for you?
   欢迎光临洗浴中心！请问您需要什么服务项目？
2. Do you have a sauna room?
   你们有桑拿浴室吗？

3. Good ideas are inspired in a good sauna bath.
   好的桑拿浴可以激发好的灵感。
4. We have a sauna bath with massage service there, too.
   在那里还有桑拿浴室并提供按摩服务。
5. After you take a sauna, you will feel relaxed.
   洗过桑拿,您会感觉很放松。
6. Her face glowed when she came out of the sauna.
   当她从桑拿浴中出来时她的脸在发光。
7. I'd like to take a sauna bath. What is your charge?
   我要洗桑拿。请问收费标准是什么?
8. Please change your slippers and take a shower first. Let me show you the way to the shower bath room.
   请您换好拖鞋,先去淋浴。让我带您去淋浴间吧。
9. May I know how many kinds of sauna bath you have?
   请问你们这里有几种蒸法?
10. The sauna bath services in our hotel include damp, dry, salt and steam bath.
    我们酒店提供湿蒸浴、干蒸浴、盐浴和水蒸浴四种桑拿浴服务。

Section B

Service Procedure 服务流程

1. Greetings.
   问候。
2. Introduce service items and facilities.
   介绍服务项目和设施。
3. Introduce the charge.
   介绍费用。
4. Examine the room card.
   检查房卡。
5. Go through the procedure.
   办手续。
6. Lead the guest to the place.
   带客人到指定位置。
7. Settle the account.

结账。

8. Bid farewell to the guest.
   道别。

Ⅰ. Service Performance 服务演练

C＝Recreation Attendant（康乐中心服务生）　　G＝Guest（客人）

C：Here are hotel's sauna rooms. Is there anything I can do for you?
这里是我们酒店的桑拿浴室。有什么需要帮助的吗？

G：I'd like to take a sauna bath. What shall I do first?
我想洗桑拿，我得先做什么？

C：For the sake of guest's health, those who have heart disease or high blood pressure are not allowed to take sauna.
考虑健康的原因，有心脏病和高血压的人是不允许洗桑拿的。

G：Thank you for telling me this. I'm in good condition.
谢谢你告诉我。我的健康状况良好。

C：First, change your shoes to slippers. Then walk up to the locker room to get prepared for a shower. After the shower, you can enter the bathroom you choose.
请您先换拖鞋，然后去更衣室准备淋浴。淋浴之后，您就可以走进您选好的桑拿间里。

G：I see. By the way, is there any difference between Finnish sauna and Turkish sauna?
我明白了。顺便问一声芬兰浴与土耳其浴有何不同？

C：The indoor temperature of Finnish bath exceeds 50℃. But the indoor temperature of the Turkish bath is not high, the marble slabs in the room are heated with warm fire, which will not make people feel uncomfortable, so it is suitable for all ages.
芬兰浴的室内温度超过50℃。而土耳其浴的室内温度不高，房间里的大理石板用温火加热，不会令人有不舒服的感觉，故老少皆宜。

G：Why should you have dry steam?
为什么要用干蒸？

C：That is to step up the blood circulation and produce vigorous perspiration. You'll be sweating. After ten minutes or so, it's time to cool off under a shower or go for a quick swim.
这是为了促进血液循环和大量排汗，会让您的汗珠一直往下淌。大约过10分钟，您就可以去冲个澡或游一会泳让自己凉快一下。

G：Sounds crazy to me.
听起来有点疯狂。

C：Actually it's fun. People usually go back into the bathroom three times.
事实上是很有意思的。通常每个人都要进去蒸三次。

G：What happens then?
洗完以后呢？

C：Then you wash yourself. And then you wrap yourself up in your sauna robe. You can have a snack, if you'd like it.
然后把自己冲洗干净。穿上浴袍，您还可以吃点小点心。

G：I see. Thank you for telling me that.
知道了。谢谢你给我介绍这些。

G：My pleasure.
很高兴为您服务。

Ⅱ. Position Practice 岗位实训

★ Introduce the price of each item. （向客人介绍各项目价格）

Can I introduce the rate for each kind of sauna?
我能向您介绍各种桑拿项目的价格吗？

★ Remind guests of the matters that they shall pay attention to when taking sauna. （提醒客人桑拿注意事项）

1. That is to step up the blood circulation and produce vigorous perspiration. You'll sweat a lot.
   它能帮人加快血液循环，使人流很多汗。您整个人就会像"汗人"一样。

2. If you feel hungry, just relax yourself by having some soft drinks and cakes at the poolside bar.
   如果您感觉饿了，就到池边的酒吧里去喝些饮料、吃点蛋糕，放松一下。

3. Please don't stay too long each time, 20 minutes at most.
   请一次不要蒸太久，最多20分钟。

★ Announce guests of settling account. （告诉客人结账事宜）

Would you please pay the bill at the service center after sauna?
请您洗完桑拿后去服务台结账，可以吗？

Ⅲ. Listening Practice 听力实训

★ A. Listen to the following passage about sauna and fill in the missing information.

Sauna has a long history. In Finland, it has at least _____ of history. Sauna is a _____ or hut heated to around _____ degrees centigrade. It is used for bathing as well as for _____ relaxation. While a hot sauna may seem a cruel punishment to _____ bathers, it is actually a very _____. All you need is a _____ and at least half an hour of time. Start with _____, and then enter the sauna for a few minutes, _____ your senses. When you've had enough, take a refreshing shower, _____ for a while and repeat _____. And there is no need to _____, it's entirely safe.

★ B. Complete the following conversation.
Attendant: Good evening, sir. _____.
Guest: Good evening. What kind of sauna do you have here?
Attendant: Ours is Finnish _____.
Guest: What's the proper temperature in the sauna?
Attendant: About 55 ℃. _____.
Guest: I see.
Attendant: Here's the key to the locker and towel.
Guest: Thank you.
(A few minutes later, the guest rushes out, sweating all over.)
Attendant: _____?
Guest: I feel quite good.
Attendant: Would you like a _____ in the sauna bar?
Guest: All right. I feel so hungry.
Attendant: This way, please.

Important 特别关注

▲ In order to reduce steam loss, please close the door as soon as you enter or exit the room.
为减少蒸汽流失，请在进出桑拿室时随手关门。

▲ Be cautious when taking sauna, those who have heart disease or high blood pressure are not allowed to take sauna, for their health's sake.
洗桑拿要注意，考虑健康原因，不允许有心脏病或高血压的人洗桑拿浴。

Section C

Case and Development 案例与创新

Case 案例

Suppose you are an inexperienced visitor to a sauna center. Ask the attendant some questions to find out what a Finnish sauna is and why sauna is good to people's health.

Development 创新

- Do you know different saunas have different effects on people?
- How should one bathe in a Finnish sauna? Describe it in your own words.
- What is a sauna and who cannot take a sauna?

技能实训 25　娱乐服务 Entertainment Service

听力音频

Section A

Basic Knowledge for Position 岗位基础知识

I. Word Stock 词库

wind brand	管乐队
string orchestra	弦乐队
light music	轻音乐
pop music	流行音乐
country music	乡村音乐
jazz music	爵士音乐
rock music	摇滚音乐
hot music	热门音乐
classical music	古典音乐
modern music	现代音乐
lyric song	抒情歌曲
folk song	民歌；山歌
love song	情歌
ballet	芭蕾舞
social dance	交谊舞
waltz	华尔兹舞
foxtrot	狐步舞
tango	探戈舞
rumba	伦巴舞
break dancing	霹雳舞
hula	草裙舞
Yangge dance	秧歌舞
discotheque	迪斯科舞厅
karaoke	卡拉 OK
private room	包间

voice	声音；嗓音
title (of a song)	歌名
stereo system	立体音响
microphone	麦克风
catalogue/list	歌单/目录
remote control	遥控器
volume	音量
Internet bar	网吧

Ⅱ. Pronunciation 语音训练

1. Minors are not allowed in.
   未成年人不得入内。

2. How many people do you have?
   你们一行一共几个人？

3. There is a minimum charge at the karaoke bar.
   卡拉OK吧设有最低消费。

4. If you are not a registered guest, you will be charged at least 100 yuan, excluding drinks.
   如果您不是住店客人，至少要收100元，不包括酒水。

5. There is a fashion show in the night club.
   夜总会有时装表演。

6. There is no entrance fee for registered guest.
   住店客人不收入场费。

7. Would you please show me your room cards?
   请出示你们的房卡。

8. Would you like something to drink?
   要不要喝点什么？

9. We have a live floor show featuring a band called Four And One.
   我们有特约的"四加一"乐队的现场表演。

10. Would you like a KTV chamber or night club hall?
    你们想要一个KTV包房还是去夜总会大厅？

11. I'd like to have a computer in the Internet bar looking for some material.
    我想在你们的网吧上网查点资料。

12. The price is more expensive than the Internet bars outside.
    这里比外面的网吧贵多了。

13. Can you use this computer? I'll switch on the computer. You can use the net by pressing this key.

    您使用这台电脑行吗？我帮您开启电脑，您只要按这个键，便可直接上网。

Section B

Service Procedure 服务流程

1. Greetings.
   问候。
2. Introduce service items and facilities.
   介绍服务项目和设施。
3. Introduce the charge.
   介绍费用。
4. Lead the guest to the place.
   带客人到指定的位置。
5. Settle account.
   结账。
6. Bid farewell to the guest.
   道别。

Ⅰ. Service Performance 服务演练

R＝Receptionist（服务员）　　A＝Andy　　C＝Christine

A：It's a nice day, isn't it?
  今天天气真好，对吧？
C：Absolutely. How about going to a karaoke bar and relax?
  绝对是的。去卡拉 OK 吧唱歌放松一下怎么样？
A：Good idea. Are there any karaoke bars nearby?
  好主意。这附近有卡拉 OK 吧吗？
C：Yeah. I know there is an excellent karaoke bar in Holiday Inn.
  有的。我知道假日酒店有一个很不错的卡拉 OK 吧。
A：It sounds great.
  好的。
  (They arrive at the hotel.)（抵达酒店）

A：Where is the karaoke bar?
卡拉 OK 吧在哪儿？

C：Maybe it is on the third floor! Oh, I'm not sure. Let me ask the receptionist. Just a minute.
可能在三楼。我不是很确定。我去问问前台服务员，稍等。
Excuse me, could you tell me the way to the karaoke bar?
打扰一下，你能告诉我卡拉 OK 吧怎么走吗？

R：Certainly. Go straight to the elevator from here and go down to the second floor. Turn left when you get out of the lift and you'll see it.
当然。从这里直走到电梯下到二楼，出了电梯后向左转就可以看到卡拉 OK 吧了。

A：Is it open now?
卡拉 OK 吧现在营业吗？

R：Yes, it opens at 9：00 p. m. and closes at 3：00 a. m.
是的。卡拉 OK 吧从晚上 9 点开到凌晨 3 点。

C：Is there anything we should take care of?
我们有需要注意的事项吗？

R：Actually, no.
没有。

C：I think we'd better get a private room. We don't want to be disturbed.
我想我们最好要一个包间。我们不想别人打扰我们。

R：It's no problem. We have a very nice private room.
没问题。我们有一个很好的包间。

A：How about the drinks here?
有饮料吗？

R：There are 30 kinds of drinks for you to choose, so you can choose any one you like.
我们提供 30 种饮料供您选择。您可以选择任何一种。

C：I heard you also provide different kinds of cocktails made by good bartenders.
我听说你们还提供由优秀的酒吧调酒员调制的各种各样的鸡尾酒。

R：Yes. That's right. What's more, you can enjoy beautiful music from the band.
是的，没错。另外，您还可以欣赏由乐队演奏的非常动听的音乐。

A：Wonderful! I cannot wait to see their performance. By the way, what's the charge?
太好了！我已经迫不及待地想看他们的表演了。顺便问一下，价格多少？

R：Are you staying at our hotel?
你们是住在我们酒店吗？

A：No.
不是。

R：According to our rules, if you are registered guests, we charge you for the drinks. If you are not, we charge 100 RMB for each private room excluding drinks.

根据我们的规定，如果你们是登记入住的客人，我们只收酒水费。如果你们不是我们的住店客人，除了收酒水费用外，每个包间我们还要收100元。

A&C：Thank you so much. We have to go now.

非常感谢。我们现在就去。

R：See you! Have a good time.

再见！希望你们玩得愉快。

Ⅱ．Position Practice 岗位实训

★ Karaoke Bar（卡拉OK吧）

1. How many people do you have?

   你们一行一共几个人？

2. There is a minimum charge at the karaoke bar.

   卡拉OK吧设有最低消费。

3. If you are not a registered guest, you will be charged at least 100 yuan, excluding drinks.

   如果您不是住店客人，至少要收100元，不包括酒水。

★ Night Club（夜总会）

1. People under 18 are not allowed in the night club.

   不满18岁不允许进入夜总会。

2. There is a fashion show in the night club.

   夜总会有时装表演。

★ Ball room（舞厅）

1. There is no entrance fee for registered guest.

   住店客人不收入场费。

2. Would you please show me your room cards?

   请出示你们的房卡。

3. Would you like something to drink?

   要不要喝点什么？

4. Will you honor me with a dance?

   请赏光跳个舞，好吗？

5. I'm engaged with this Tango.

   已经有人约我跳探戈舞了。

★ Mahjong's room（麻将室）

1. Mahjong is a traditional Chinese recreational activity.

   麻将是中国传统的娱乐活动。

2. Mahjong is somewhat like playing cards.
   玩麻将有点像打扑克牌。
3. Playing Mahjong is very time-consuming.
   玩麻将很消耗时间。

Ⅲ. Listening Practice 听力实训

★ A. Listen to the following passage about entertainment and fill in the missing information.

Most hotels and resorts have outstanding _____ and entertainment, guests may find plenty of options for the _____. Some guests can dance and _____ after a busy day of sightseeing. Others may listen to the _____ or enjoy a good _____. If hotels don't have the _____ entertainment facilities, when the sun goes down and the guests may head out for the night, exploring _____ or just watching the sunset with an icy _____, these places are probably within _____ or quick drive. Dazzling and gentle lighting brings the guests into _____, making the guests too delighted to leave in the nightlife.

★ B. Complete the following conversation.

Attendant: Good evening, sir. _____.

Guest: Good evening. A table in the corner, please.

Attendant: Yes. This way, please... Please take your seat. _____?

Guest: Lemon juice, please.

Attendant: All right. Just a minute... _____.

Guest: What beautiful music! Would you like to have a dance with me, Miss?

Attendant: I'd be glad to, _____.

Guest: All right. To tell the truth, you are the prettiest girl I've ever met.

Attendant: Thank you for saying so.

Guest: Can we be friends?

Attendant: Yes, _____. But I don't know your name.

Guest: Fox. And yours?

Attendant: Lisa Wang.

(Mr. Fox is about to leave.)

Guest: Lisa. This is for you. Your service is excellent.

Attendant: Thank you, Mr. Fox. _____.

Guest: Goodbye.

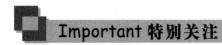

▲ Please use the equipments in the Internet bar carefully according to the regulations. Any damages caused by misuse should be compensated.
请按照操作规范使用网吧设备，凡因人为使用不当所造成的损坏均须按酒店规定予以赔偿。

▲ If you encounter any problems when you are running the computer, please ask our staff for help. Don't change or delete data of the computer by yourselves.
上网时，若遇到疑难问题，请咨询服务人员帮忙解决。不得改变或删除电脑数据。

▲ Please don't listen, watch and copy unhealthy contents which are obscene or superstitious and other illegal contents in the Internet bar. Doing anything that has nothing to do with the service contents is not allowed.
不得在网吧收听、收看、拷贝淫秽、迷信等不健康的内容及其他违法内容。不得在网吧从事与服务内容无关的其他任何活动。

Section C

Case and Development 案例与创新

Case 案例

A group of young people enter a Karaoke bar to hold a birthday party. The waitress is receiving them.

Development 创新

• If there is a minimum charge at the karaoke bar, should you inform the guests in advance?
• How should you explain to young people under 18 when they want to enter the night club?
• Are drinks free of charge for the registered guest at the ball room?

实训模块六

购物服务
Shopping Service

Shopping arcade is an important composition of a hotel. Hotels for foreigners always offer shopping arcades to meet the need of the in-house guests and meanwhile gain economic benefits. An attendant in a shopping mall needs to equip himself with not only a fairly good command of a foreign language, friendliness and politeness, but also the knowledge of the goods he sells. He has to provide the guests with a proper introduction, and give them a pleasant shopping experience during the tour.

商场是酒店经营的一个重要组成部分。涉外酒店大多设有商场，在满足住店客人的需要的同时，也获得经济效益。商场的服务员在具有较好的外语交际能力的基础上，不仅要友好礼貌地对待客人，而且需要对自己所销售的商品有足够的了解，能够向客人进行恰到好处的介绍，以方便游客在游玩的闲暇中享受购物的乐趣。

技能实训 26　旅游纪念品 Souvenir

Section A

Basic Knowledge for Position 岗位基础知识

Ⅰ. Word Stock 词库

antique shop	古玩店
antique	古玩
bracelet	镯子
brooch	胸针
calligraphy	书法
bracelet	手链
change	零钱
cosmetics	化妆用品
electric razor	电动剃须刀
crystal	水晶
earring	耳环
free of charge	不收费
genuine	真的
jewelry	珠宝；首饰
gold jewelry	金饰
silver jewelry	银饰
imitation	仿制品
necklace	项链
pearl	珍珠
porcelain	瓷器
price tag	标价签
ring	戒指
shop assistant/salesman	售货员
display window	橱窗
silk fan	绢扇
silk flower	绢花

silk painting	绢画
souvenir	纪念品
deliver	送
keep the bill	留发票
wrap up	包装

Ⅱ. Pronunciation 语音训练

1. China is the homeland of giant pandas, so this T-shirt with a lovely panda on it could be an ideal gift for your friends.
   中国是大熊猫的故乡,所以印有熊猫图案的T恤是送给您朋友理想的礼物。

2. The artists can produce various kinds of paper-cuts, like human figures, landscapes, flowers, birds, etc.
   艺术家可以剪不同形状的纸,如人物、风景、花朵、鸟类等。

3. Paper-cut of Yangzhou has created a unique artistic style and distinctive local features.
   扬州剪纸创造了独特的艺术风格和鲜明的地方特色。

4. You have an excellent shape. Cheongsam is so popular with young ladies nowadays in China.
   您的身材非常好。如今旗袍在中国很受年轻女士的欢迎。

5. It might be a little expensive, but the material is of the best quality, and our workmanship is the best in the city. It's of great worth.
   这件衣服也许有点贵,但用料上乘,而且我们的工艺在这个城市是最好的,非常有价值。

6. What color do you think is the most suitable for me?
   你认为哪种颜色适合我?

7. Will you please let me have a close look at the silk fabrics?
   能让我仔细看看这块真丝面料吗?

8. The suit looks terrific on you. Would you like to take it?
   这套西装穿在您身上很棒。您要买它吗?

9. I'd like to buy some seals. Would you please show me some for selection?
   我想买几块石章。你能拿一些让我挑选吗?

10. This is exactly the Yixing clay teapot that he has dreamed of for many years.
    这正是他多年来梦寐以求的紫砂壶。

Section B

Service Procedure 服务流程

1. Greetings.
   问候。
2. Find out the information the guest wants.
   了解客人所需的信息。
3. Recommend or introduce products to the guest.
   向客人介绍产品。
4. Praise the products that the guest chooses.
   称赞客人挑选的产品。
5. Tell the guest where and how to pay.
   告诉客人去哪里以及怎么样付款。
6. Bid farewell to the guest.
   道别。

I. Service Performance 服务演练

A＝Shop Assistant（商场服务员）　　G＝Guest（客人）

A：Can I help you?
　　需要帮助吗?

G：I want to find something typically Chinese to decorate my room.
　　我想买有典型中国特色的东西装饰我的房间。

A：How about this artistic tapestry and this cloisonne vase?
　　这个艺术挂毯和这个景泰蓝花瓶怎么样?

G：Well, I am looking for something special. These teapots are beautiful. The color is similar to that of my living room. Are they made of porcelain?
　　我想买一些特别的东西。这些茶具很漂亮, 颜色和我的客厅的颜色很相近。它们是瓷制的吗?

A：No, they are made of clay. They are Yixing clay teapots. This kind of tea ware is very famous in China.
　　不是的。它们是由黏土做成的, 是紫砂壶。这种茶具在中国很有名。

G：Ah, I see. How can I make tea with this teapot?
　　哦, 知道了。用这个茶具怎么泡茶?

A：That depends on what kind of tea you want to make. The Chinese tea is classified into green tea, white tea, oolong tea, black tea, Pu'er tea, scented tea, etc. What kind of tea do you like?

这取决于你要泡什么茶。中国茶分为绿茶、白茶、乌龙茶、红茶、普洱茶和花茶等。您想喝什么茶？

G：Well, I am a little familiar with black tea. Can you show me how to make the tea?

哦，我比较熟悉红茶。你能泡给我看吗？

A：I am sorry to say we do not have any tea in this shop, but I can tell you the steeping method. First, put the tea leaves into the pot, then pour hot water into it, the amount of tea in proportion to water is 1 to 9. The temperature of the water is 100℃. After 10 seconds, the tea is ready.

对不起，我们店里现在没有茶叶。但我可以教您浸泡的方法。首先，把茶叶放入茶壶中，然后加上开水，茶叶和水的比例是1∶9。水的温度是100℃。10秒钟后，茶就泡好了。

G：Thanks. What is the price of this tea set?

多谢，这套茶具价格是多少？

A：It is 600 yuan.

价格是600元。

G：That's too much, I will take it if you give me a 40％ discount.

太贵了。如果你给我打6折，我就买一些。

A：Well, I can just take 100 yuan off the price.

哦，我只能给您减掉100元。

G：All right, I will take this set.

好的，我买了。

A：Anything else for you?

您还需要其他的吗？

G：Yes, what is on this paper cut?

是的。这个剪纸是什么？

A：They are lotus flowers.

是荷花。

G：Ah, how beautiful! How much is it?

哦，真漂亮！多少钱？

A：It is 20 yuan.

20元。

G：I will take it as well. Can I have it framed? I want to hang it up in the bedroom.

这个我也买了。能帮我做个镜框吗？我想把它挂在卧室里。

A：Yes，but you will have to pay for the frame. It is 30 yuan.
　　　　好的。但您得付镜框的钱，30元。
　　G：All right. Here is the money. It is 550 yuan altogether.
　　　　好的。给你钱。一共是550元。
　　A：Thank you.
　　　　谢谢。
　　G：Would you give me a shopping bag?
　　　　你能给我一个购物袋吗？
　　A：Yes，here you are.
　　　　当然，给您。

Ⅱ. Position Practice 岗位实训

★ Introduce different tea to the guest.（向客人介绍不同的茶）

1. The top-grade Longjing Tea is manually baked. It is fresh green with a strong aroma.
   极品龙井茶是手工焙制的。它色泽碧绿，香味特别浓郁。
2. Anhui Tieguanyin is fine both in appearance and in quality, and it has a weight-loss effect.
   安徽铁观音无论外观还是质量均属上乘，而且它具有减肥的功效。
3. It's a high-quality green tea mixed with dried jasmine flowers.
   这种绿茶质量高，里面有晒干的茉莉花。

★ Introduce "Four Treasures of the Study" to the guest.（向客人介绍"文房四宝"）

　　"Four Treasures of the Study" are the four stationery items indispensable to any traditional Chinese scholars, which include the brush, ink, paper, and ink stone.
　　"文房四宝"指的是古代中国学者不可缺少的书房用具：笔、墨、纸、砚。

★ Introduce different paintings.（介绍不同的画）

　　Briefly speaking, western oil paintings are created by colors and brush touches while traditional Chinese paintings are by lines and strokes.
　　简单地说，西方油画是由颜色和油画笔画出来的，而传统中国画是由线条勾勒一笔一笔画出来的。

实训模块六　购物服务　Shopping Service

Ⅲ. Listening Practice 听力实训

★ A. Listen to the following passage about souvenirs and fill in the missing information.

Millions of foreigners and _____ Chinese visit the mainland of China every year _____, _____, or exchanges in different fields. Many of them return home loaded with _____. Souvenirs are precious _____ for most tourists. Some guests will buy T-shirts, key chains, _____ or any candies that are native to a place. Others may buy some _____ from a native city or some souvenirs with the name of the city on it. _____ are also a good choice as souvenirs. It is a way to remember the _____ places. Guests can _____ souvenirs for themselves, their family and friends.

★ B. Complete the following conversation.

们考虑的要素之一，但不宜过分强调。

▲ If the guest says: "I'm just having a look." This means they want to choose the goods they prefer in no hurry without being intervened.
如果客人说："我只是看看。"说明他们不想被关注，希望自己慢慢挑选合意的商品。

▲ If the goods which the guest has bought are antiques and valuables, the shop assistant needs to remind him to keep the receipt or invoice well in case it is inspected by the customs.
如果客人购买的是古玩或特别贵重的物品，还需要提醒客人保存好收据或发票，以备海关查验。

Section C

Case and Development 案例与创新

Case 案例

A guest comes into your shopping arcade to look for a carpet for his friend. You are the shop assistant there. Try your best to give the guest a detailed introduction of your products. The guest shows great interest in a certain carpet. However, he begins to bargain for it.

Development 创新

• What kind of souvenirs are most attractive to visitors in China?

• Your guest finally decides that she's not going to buy any of the souvenirs which you have shown her. How do you help her to withdraw gracefully?

• Under what circumstances cannot the guests be refunded for what they have bought in the shopping arcade?

技能实训 27　当地特产 Local Specialty

Section A

Basic Knowledge for Position 岗位基础知识

I. Word Stock 词库

local specialty	当地特产
silk	蚕丝
satin	绸缎
brocade	织锦
silk product	丝绸产品
silk scarf	丝绸围巾
dry cleaning	干洗
iron	熨
bedspread	床罩
quilt cover	被套
folding fan	折叠扇
silk umbrella	丝绸伞
bamboo products	竹制品
preserved fruit	果脯
handicraft	手工艺品
carving	雕刻
scissors	剪刀
embroidery	刺绣
carpet	地毯
Beijing crisp candy	北京酥糖
block printing	木版画
compared with	与……比较
cultural atmosphere	文化氛围
delicate appearance	精致的外观
exquisite workmanship	工艺精巧

🔊 Ⅱ. Pronunciation 语音训练

1. Silk products are very popular among tourists.
   丝绸产品非常受游客的欢迎。
2. What size would you like to have?
   您要多大的尺寸?
3. Please wash it by hand with special detergent for silk washing and rinse it well.
   手洗时请放一定量的真丝洗涤剂,然后用清水漂洗。
4. I wonder if the color will fade in washing.
   我想知道这种颜色在洗涤中会不会褪色。
5. Do you have T-shirts with words "Beijing Olympics" printed on them?
   你有没有印有"北京奥运会"字样的 T 恤衫?
6. As a matter of fact, all the T-shirts here are both colorfast and shrink-proof.
   事实上,这里所有的 T 恤衫都不褪色,并且防缩水。
7. I'd like to buy a dress closely related to Chinese culture as a souvenir for my trip in China.
   我想买一件具有中国文化特色的衣服,作为我中国之行的留念。
8. By the way, the silk shouldn't be hung out in the sunshine.
   顺便提醒您,真丝不能放在阳光下曝晒。

Section B

Service Procedure 服务流程

1. Greetings.
   问候。
2. Find out what the guest wants.
   了解客人需要什么。
3. Recommend specialty to the guest.
   向客人介绍特产。
4. Praise the products that the guest chooses.
   称赞客人挑选的产品。
5. Tell the guest where and how to pay.
   告诉客人去哪里以及怎么样付款。
6. Bid farewell to the guest.
   与客人道别。

Ⅰ. Service Performance 服务演练

A= Shop Assistant（商场服务员）　　G= Guest（客人）

A：Good afternoon, madam. Can I help you?
女士，下午好。有什么需要帮忙的吗？

G：Yes. I'm looking for a silk shirt for my husband. Would you show me some, please?
是的。我想给我的丈夫买一件真丝衬衣。能拿一件给我看看吗？

A：Certainly. We have a wide selection of silk shirts here. But what size, please?
当然。我们这里有很多真丝衬衣供您挑选。您要什么型号的？

G：Large.
大号。

A：How do you like these?
这几件怎么样？

G：How nice! They all look beautiful. But the problem is that I'm not good at choosing. I wonder if you could help me.
很好啊！看起来都很漂亮。但问题是我不太会挑选。你能帮我挑吗？

A：Yes, with pleasure. By feeling them with hands, I can assure you that these shirts are of good quality. They are made of silk with super texture. I would recommend the purple one. It is the fashionable color this year. I'm sure that your husband would be very happy to have such an excellent gift.
好的，很高兴为您服务。用手摸摸，我可以向您保证这些衬衣的质量很好。它们是上好的真丝面料制成的。我向您推荐紫色的这件。今年很流行紫色，我敢保证您丈夫将非常高兴收到这份礼物。

G：Thank you very much. By the way, does it fade?
非常感谢。随便问一下，不褪色吧？

A：No, it doesn't fade and it is washable. But I would suggest that you wash by hand. Please don't rub. Just use soapy water and rinse well.
不褪色，可以水洗的。但我建议您手洗，不要用手搓，仅用肥皂水漂洗就可以了。

G：Right then, I would like to buy it. How much is it?
好的，那我买了。这件多少钱？

A：The price tag says two hundred and eighty yuan.
标签上是280元。

G：That is more than I expected to pay. Shall I see a cheaper one of the same quality?
太贵了。能给我看一件同等质量的便宜一点的吗？

A：I'm afraid not. In my opinion, it is worthwhile because of its good quality, though a bit expensive. It is a good gift for your husband. But anyway, you have all the right to make your own decision.

可能没有了。我认为虽然这件贵一点，但质量很好，是一件送给您丈夫很好的礼物。但不管怎么说，您可以再考虑考虑。

G：All right, I might take it. Thank you very much for your help.

那好，我买一件。感谢你的帮助。

Ⅱ. Position Practice 岗位实训

★ Introduce Hangzhou silk to the guest. （向客人介绍杭州丝绸）

Silk is the symbol of the oriental culture and it represents the specialty and tradition of Hangzhou. Silk products include silk clothes, artworks, tourist souvenirs, neckties, scarves and various other silk products. These products have both consumers at home and abroad.

丝绸是东方文化的象征，它代表了杭州的特色和传统。杭州的丝绸产品包括真丝服装、艺术品、旅游纪念品、领带、丝巾和各种各样的真丝面料。这些产品不仅有本国的消费群体，还有海外的消费群体。

★ Make sure what kind of style the guest would like. （确认客人喜欢的款式）

1. How do you like the style? / What do you think of the style?

   您觉得这个款式怎么样？

2. This style is in fashion this year.

   这个款式今年很流行。

3. The style is popular with foreign guests.

   外国客人很喜欢这个款式。

4. The style is out of fashion/out of date now.

   这个款式现在过时了。

★ Make sure what color the guest would like. （确认客人喜欢的颜色）

1. What color do you like?

   您喜欢什么颜色？

2. What's your favorite color?

   您最喜欢什么颜色？

3. Which color do you prefer, pink or orange?

   您喜欢哪种颜色，粉红的还是橙色的？

4. This color is quite in fashion this year.

   今年这种颜色很流行。

5. The color goes well with the skirt.

   这种颜色跟裙子很匹配。

★ Different ways to greet the guest. （招呼客人的不同方式）

1. Excuse me. Can I help you? / What can I do for you?

   能够为您服务吗？

2. Hello. Are you being attended to? Can I help you?

您好，有人招呼您吗？能够帮您什么？

3. Could I serve you?

能够为您效劳吗？

★ Make recommendations to the guest.（向客人介绍产品）

1. What about/ How about this one?

这件怎么样？

2. Which style do you prefer?

您喜欢什么款式？

3. Do you like this design?

这款设计您喜欢吗？

4. What color and size do you want?

您要什么样的颜色和尺寸？

★ Seeing a guest off.（送别客人）

You are welcome. / Hope to see you again. / Have a good day.

不客气！/欢迎再次光临！/祝您过得愉快！

Ⅲ. Listening Practice 听力实训

★ A. Listen to five short conversations in shopping arcade and mark "√" where appropriate.

	Food Stuff	Garments	Medicine	Jewelry	Arts &Crafts
Dialogue 1					
Dialogue 2					
Dialogue 3					
Dialogue 4					
Dialogue 5					

★ B. Complete the following conversation.

Assistant：Good afternoon, sir. _____. May I help you?

Guest：Good afternoon. The shop is well-decorated.

Assistant：Thank you. _____?

Guest：Yes, I hear that porcelain in China is fascinating, isn't it?

Assistant：That's right. You _____.

Guest：Thank you. This set of tableware is of perfect traditional Chinese design, do you think so?

　　Assistant：Yes，indeed. _____ . It's made in Jingdezhen，"the capital of porcelain."

　　Guest：How much is it?

　　Assistant：＄260. _____ .

　　Guest：Great! I'll take this set.

 Important 特别关注

▲ When the guest enters a shop，what we should do is just to introduce the items，but we cannot persuade him to buy anything.
进入商店后，我们应该做的是向客人介绍商品，不能劝客人购物。

▲ When guests do the shopping，we should keep the principle of honesty.
客人进商场购物时，我们应本着诚信的原则。

Section C

Case and Development 案例与创新

Case 案例

　　Mr. and Mrs. Ashmore come to your store to buy some silk products. But they don't know how to choose. Show them what you have in the store and give them some advice on what and how to choose.

Development 创新

　　• An British woman is looking for a baby's dress. A shop assistant shows her the samples and explains the quality, size and styles.

　　• You are a shop assistant. You are now discussing with a guest about her preference of light color. How can you give her some suggestions?

　　• Why would most guests like to buy some local specialties?

实训模块七

会展服务
Convention and Exhibition

This section focuses on the function of banqueting and convention department, especially on the working skills of hotel staff required on occasions such as convention reservation, convention registration and exhibition arrangement.

本模块介绍宴会和会议部中会展服务的功能，尤其关注酒店工作人员在会务预订、会议代表签到和展览安排中涉及的工作技能。

技能实训 28　会议服务 Convention Service

Section A

Basic Knowledge for Position 岗位基础知识

I. Word Stock 词库

convention	（从业者、政党成员等的）大会，集会
conference	（通常持续几天的大型正式）会议，研讨会
plenary session	全体成员会议
seminar	（大学教师带领学生作专题讨论的）研讨课；培训会
product launch	新产品发布会
board meeting	理事会
forum	论坛；讨论会
panel	专家咨询组
training session	培训会议
boardroom	董事会会议室
function room	多功能厅
multimedia	多媒体
prospectus	简介
attendee	与会者
venue	会议地点；展览地点
side curtain	边幕
curtain	幕布
laptop	手提电脑
keynoter	主演讲者
lectern	演讲台
projector	投影
video conference	视频会议
lapel microphone	领夹式话筒
sponsor	主办单位；赞助者
convention service manager	会议服务经理

Ⅱ. Pronunciation 语音训练

1. How many participants will be in the conference?
   一共有多少人参加会议？
2. What kind of room would you like for the conference?
   你们需要哪种类型的会议室？
3. Do you have any special demands for the conference facilities?
   你们对会议设施有何特殊要求？
4. Do you have any special demands for the conference service?
   你们对会议服务有何特殊要求？
5. Shall we confirm the details of the service and facilities?
   我们确认一下服务和设施的细节好吗？
6. How would you like to make payment, sir?
   先生，请问你们用何种方式付款？
7. Besides the service guidance and the price list of the services of our hotel, I'll send you a plan of the actual conference center.
   除了本酒店的服务指南和服务价目单以外，我还给您传一张会议中心的平面图。
8. Could you tell me your requirements for catering of the conference?
   请问您对会议的餐饮安排有什么要求？
9. The suppers on the first day and last day of the conference are banquets. Other meals are buffets.
   会议的第一天和最后一天的晚餐为宴会。其他时间采用自助餐。
10. Here is your meeting badge and meeting packet.
    这是您的会议徽章和会议资料袋。

Section B

Service Procedure 服务流程

1. Make a reservation of the meeting.
   预订会议。
2. Discuss the service details of the meeting.
   讨论会议服务细节。
3. Show facilities and the decoration of the meeting hall.
   向预订会议者展示会议设施和会议厅装饰。

4. Register for the conference.
   会议登记。

5. Routine service.
   日常服务。

6. Check the rental equipments.
   检查租用的设备。

7. Payment/Pay the bill.
   付账。

I. Service Performance 服务演练

S=Susan（苏珊）　　H=Hilton（希尔顿）

S：Shanghai Convention Center. How can I help you?
  这里是上海会议中心，我能为您服务吗？

H：I'm calling from New York Export Company. I wonder if I'd hold a conference in your place.
  我是纽约出口公司。我想了解是否能在你们那儿举办会议。

S：I'd be glad to help you. For how many people, sir?
  很高兴为您服务。先生，会议有多少人参加？

H：300.
  300人。

S：When will the event be held?
  会议什么时候召开？

H：October the 16th, the 17th and the 18th.
  从10月16—18日。

S：Let me have a check, please. Sorry to have kept you waiting, sir. We do have vacant suites and conference hall during the period you desire for.
  我帮您查一下……先生，对不起，让您久等了。在这个时间段里，我们有空余的套房和会议室。

H：That's good. Our attendees are all famous people. Is it possible that they each have a suite?
  好。与会人员都是些名人。每人一间套房可以吗？

S：Don't worry, sir. Since ours is an all-suite convention center, every attendee is offered a suite and VIP treatment.
  先生，别担心。因为我们的酒店是全套房的会议中心，所以我们会给每位客人提供一间套房，客人享受的都是贵宾级待遇。

H：I like that very much. Then what is the rate?
  太好了。价格如何？

S: We offer competitive prices, just like other standard hotel, 1080 RMB per person per day, equal to 150 US dollars. Besides, we also offer complimentary breakfast and afternoon tea.
我们的价格和普通酒店的价格差不多，每人每天人民币1080元，也就是150美元。另外，我们还提供免费的早餐和下午茶。

H: Great. Sounds reasonable. We can enjoy suite service. Everybody's dream!
很好。听起来很合理。我们可以享受套房的待遇。这是每个人的梦想！

S: Exactly, sir. Our homely atmosphere will realize your dream. If you are really interested in our center, I'll send you a reservation form and a prospectus about our meeting facilities.
是的，先生。我们营造的家一般的氛围将使你们梦想成真。如果你们有意入住我们的酒店，我将发一个预订单和一份关于我们会议中心设施的说明书给您。

H: That's very kind of you. Can you send them by fax?
好的。能传真给我吗？

S: Yes, sir. May I have your name and your fax number?
好的，先生。能告诉我您的名字和传真号吗？

H: John Hilton, H-I-L-T-O-N. My fax number is 708682-3352.
约翰·希尔顿，H-I-L-T-O-N。我的传真号是708682-3352。

S: Mr. Hilton. Your fax number is 708682-3352. Yes, I'll make it right away.
希尔顿先生，您的传真号是708682-3352。我马上就给您发传真。

H: Thank you very much. Goodbye.
非常感谢！再见。

S: Goodbye, Mr. Hilton. Thanks for calling.
再见，希尔顿先生。感谢您的来电。

Ⅱ. Position Practice 岗位实训

★ Obtain the information of reservation. （预订会议时要了解下列信息）

1. What size of the conference or how many participants.
   会议规模或参加会议的人数。
2. What kind of conference or what kind of function room.
   会议类型或需要具有何种功能的会议室。
3. The special demands for the meeting facilities.
   对会议设施的特殊要求。
4. The special demands for the meeting service.
   对会议服务的特殊要求。
5. The time of the conference.
   会议的时间。

6. The number of the rooms needed.
   房间数量。

7. Discussion of the service details of the meeting.
   讨论会议服务的细节。

★ Confirm the following details with the meeting planner.（与会议策划人确认以下细节）

1. The number of the participants.
   与会人数。

2. The number and the size of the conference rooms.
   所需的不同大小的会议室的间数。

3. The facilities for the meeting.
   所需的会议设施。

4. The arrangements and demands for catering of the meeting.
   会议餐饮安排和要求。

5. The demands in detail for the meeting services and meeting facilities.
   会议服务的细节要求和会议设施的要求。

6. The number of the rooms and the room rates.
   房间数和房价。

7. The food and beverage rates.
   餐饮费用。

8. Ways of payment.
   付款方式。

Ⅲ. Listening Practice 听力实训

★ A. Listen to the following passage about convention and fill in the missing information.

A convention center or conference center is a _____ that is designed to _____ a convention, where individuals and groups _____ to promote and _____ common interests. Convention centers typically _____ sufficient floor area to accommodate _____ attendees. Very large venues, suitable for major _____, are sometimes known as _____. Convention centers typically have at least one auditorium and may also contain concert halls, _____, meeting rooms, and _____. Some large resort area hotels _____ a convention center.

★ B. Complete the following conversation.

Manager: Hello. _____.

Guest: Me too. I'm here to discuss with you about holding a meeting at your hotel.

Manager: _____. What meeting is it?

Guest: An annual convention of the Writers Association.

Manager: _____?

Guest: Certainly. Here it is.

Manager: Oh, I see. There are 50 attendees. I think our function room _____ _____.

Guest: Do you have enough brainstorming rooms? We have several seminars after the lecture.

Manager: Don't worry. We'll reorganize some rooms _____.

Guest: Shall we discuss some details about meeting facilities?

Manager: Here are the convention brochures _____ about meeting facilities.

Guest: Thank you. We'll let you know as soon as we've decided.

Important 特别关注

▲ Since the customer is the most important asset of a company, any conference should be well organised. Among all aspects, the location of the conference venue is of utmost importance.
客户是公司最重要的资产，任何会议都应该有序组织。在组织会议时，会议场所位置的选择是至关重要的。

▲ The conference venue should be selected based on its location, services and reputation. It is important that it should be organised in a well-known and relatively central location.
会议场所的选择应考虑它的地理位置、服务和信誉，重要的是它应该选在一个著名且相对中心的地方。

▲ Entertaining and hosting the guests with good food and drink is also important. Customers feel valued if they are hospitably received.
使客人感到快乐和用美食招待客人同样很重要。如果你热情招待了客人，他们会觉得自己很受重视。

Section C

Case and Development 案例与创新

Case 案例

Suppose you are the planner for the World Tourism Seminar which will be held next year and last 3 days. There will be 300 attendees and the venue will be in the Shangri-La Hotel. You go to the hotel to make a site inspection about its facilities. A sales clerk receives you and introduces all the facilities you need.

Development 创新

- What is included in a conference packet?
- What is the duty of a convention service manager?
- Why is the convention business very profitable for the hotel industry?

技能实训 29　展览服务 Exhibition Service

听力音频

Section A

Basic Knowledge for Position 岗位基础知识

I. Word Stock 词库

auditorium	礼堂，会堂
high-tech	高科技
presenter/speaker	演讲人/发言人
sight	视线
laptop	手提电脑
heating	供暖
slide presentation	幻灯演示
recreational amenities	娱乐设施
parking lot	停车场
conference table	会议桌
set-up and tear-down	布置和撤台
function room charge	会议室费用
advance set-up	提前布置
late tear-down	拖后撤台
cost of labor	人工费用
meeting activity book	会议活动簿
procedure manual	工作程序手册
foldable equipment	可折叠设备
round table	圆桌
conference name/event name	会议名称/活动名称
conference room name	会议室名称
setup	布局
facility name	设施名称
facility sample	设施样板
display table	展示桌
buffet table	自助餐桌

II. Pronunciation 语音训练

1. May I know what kind of the exhibition it is?
   能告诉我这是哪种类型的展览吗?
2. How many participants will be there in the exhibition?
   会有多少人来参加展览?
3. Do you have any special requirements for the exhibition?
   您对展览有什么特殊的要求吗?
4. We need some writing desks or places for materials.
   我们需要一个供书写的桌子或摆放资料的地方。
5. This may mean that the speaker or panel needs to be located in a higher platform.
   也就是说,发言人或发言小组应该位于一个高一点的平台上。
6. Chairs are lined up in rows, facing the speaker or focal point in the room.
   椅子成行排列,面对发言人或会议室的中心。
7. This format can take several shapes, which include closed layout with no center aisle, and open layout which has rows with aisles to provide easy access to seats.
   这种布局有好几种形式,包括没有中间走道的封闭式布局和有走道便于寻找座位的开放式布局。
8. We have modern facilities and first-class service for the exhibition.
   我们有现代化的展览设施和一流的服务。

Section B

Service Procedure 服务流程

1. Book an exhibition.
   预订展览。
2. Discuss about the exhibition.
   讨论展览事宜。
3. Set up the booths.
   搭建展台。
4. Serve during the exhibition.
   展览期间服务。
5. Tear down the booths.
   拆展台。

6．Make the payment.
付款。

Ⅰ．Service Performance 服务演练

G＝Guest（客人）　　　C＝Clerk（服务生）

C：Glad to see you, Mr. Brown.
布朗先生，很高兴见到您。

G：Glad to see you, too, Miss Wang. Have you begun the work?
王小姐，见到你我也很高兴。你们开始工作了吗？

C：Yes, we've made the preparation. Let's go to the exhibition halls. This is the north exhibition hall and that's the south exhibition hall. How can we arrange the exhibition halls?
开始了，我们已做好准备了。我们到展厅去吧。这里是北展厅，那里是南展厅。我们怎么安排展厅呢？

G：The gate of the north exhibition hall is decorated as the entrance of the international exhibition for silk. The north exhibition hall is arranged as the exhibition hall for the silk materials, and the silk products are shown in the south exhibition hall.
北展厅的大门入口处布置成此次国际丝绸展的入口。北展厅展出丝绸面料，南展厅展出丝绸制品。

C：We have the same idea. It's convenient for us to carry those big stools to the exhibition hall from the storehouse. How can we deal with the two rooms?
我们的想法一样。从仓库搬那些大型的工具去展厅也方便。这两间房间怎么布置呢？

G：The east room is used as our exhibition office, and the west one is for the negotiation. The trade negotiation and contracts signing can be carried out here.
东边的房间作为我们的展览办公室；西边的房间作为洽谈室，贸易洽谈、签合同都在这里进行。

C：How about setting up the stands? The exhibitors of silk materials are more than those of silk products.
怎样布置展台呢？丝绸面料的参展商要比丝绸制品的参展商多。

G：The material booths are arranged in the shape of a peninsula, while the product booths are fixed up in the shape of an island.
材料展台布置成半岛形，成品展台布置成岛形。

C：Would you like some flowers and plants to decorate the booths and the halls?
展台和大厅需要用鲜花和绿色植物来装饰吗？

G：Certainly.

当然需要。

C：Will you provide some snacks and beverages for the visitors?
为参观者提供小吃和饮料吗?

G：Yes, we plan to provide some free snacks and mineral water for the visitors.
是的,我们计划提供一些免费的小吃和矿泉水。

C：Food and beverage service is at the corridor connecting the two halls.
餐饮服务就设在两个大厅的过道上。

G：It's a good idea.
好主意。

C：Are there any other suggestions and demands for our work?
对我们的工作还有什么建议或要求吗?

G：No.
没有了。

C：Could you come to inspect our work at 10 o'clock in the morning of October 26?
10月26日上午10点您能过来检查我们的工作吗?

G：Yes, I will. See you in two days.
能,我会来的。两天以后见。

C：See you.
再见。

Ⅱ. Position Practice 岗位实训

★ Get the following information in reservation.(预订展览时获取下列信息)

1. The size of the exhibition hall.
   所需展厅的大小。

2. The number of the participants.
   参展商的人数。

3. The number of the visitors.
   看展的人数。

4. The kind of exhibits and special demands for the exhibition hall.
   展品的类型和展品对展厅的要求。

5. Whether a storehouse is needed or not and what is size of it.
   是否需要仓库,以及所需仓库的大小。

6. The demands for the exhibition service.
   对展览服务的要求。

7. The special demands for the clerks who will take part in setting up the exhibition service.

对布展员工的特殊要求。

8. The time of the conference.
   展会的时间。

★ Introduce the facilities and services of the hotel.（介绍酒店的会议设施和服务）
We have modern facilities and first-class service for conference.
我们拥有现代化的会议设施和一流的会议服务。

★ Get the name of the exhibition planner and his telephone number.（获得布展商的姓名、电话号码）
May I have your name and telephone number, sir?
先生，能告诉我您的名字和电话号码吗？

Ⅲ. Listening Practice 听力实训

★ A. Listen to the following passage about convention and fill in the missing information.

There are many different kinds of _____. Some exhibitions are displayed for _____ of time such as _____ or art galleries. In some cases, like traveling exhibitions or _____, space may be rented for this _____ in similar buildings or in a more commercial setting. Exhibitions of this kind can be divided into _____. They are cultural exhibitions, commercial-cultural exhibitions and _____ displays. The most _____ one in an exhibition center is company display. Company displays can be found in _____, _____ or display cases. These are commercial exhibitions.

★ B. Complete the following conversation.

Manager: Good morning. _____!

Guest: Good morning. I'd like to confirm the details of the coming exhibition in person.

Manager: Sure. The exhibition is to be held _____, for two days. Is that right?

Guest: Yes, that's right. And how many people can you hold in your exhibition hall? We have about 500 attendees.

Manager: _____. Our exhibition hall can hold 1000 people.

Guest: Oh, that's good.

Manager: Do you have any _____ about the exhibition hall?

Guest: Yes. As for the light, I think the hall should be _____.

Manager: Sure, no problem.

Guest: We also need some flowers and green plants.

Manager: Yes. The flowers and plants can help to _____ atmosphere.
Guest: Thank you. You are always helpful.

Important 特别关注

▲ Determine the goals, problems, stand type and location of your exhibition.
确定展览的目标和问题以及展览的类型和展位。

▲ Do not forget to confirm with the exhibition manager the schedule of exhibits delivery and unloading ahead of time, because the installation and setting-up of the large-scale equipment takes more time.
一定要提前和展览经理确认展品交货、卸货的时间,因为安装大型设备往往需要很多时间。

▲ It is necessary to organize stand cleaning. The dust and fingerprints will ruin your stand. In general, the organizers will clean the passage, but you have to take responsibility of stand yourself.
非常有必要组织展位清洁工作。展位上的灰尘和指纹会让你的展位大打折扣。通常,主办单位要清理通道,但你必须要对自己的展台负责。

Section C

Case and Development 案例与创新

Case 案例

The exhibition was planned to open at 9 o'clock on the morning of October 26. At 8:10, everything was ready. But at that time, the exhibition planner Mr. Harry Brown came to the manager's office in a hurry with two exhibitors. They complained that the presentation table you arranged for them was too small.

Development 创新

• If the facilities and services you supply don't meet the need of the exhibition, how can you solve the problem?

• Will you get in touch with the guests after the exhibition comes to an end, why or why not?

• What will you do if you want to turn potential customers into regular customers?

实训模块八

投诉
Complaints

Some complaints may be reasonable. Some complaints may not be your fault. But it's usually best to apologize to the guest and take steps. In a service industry, the customer is always right (even if he or she is wrong). An apology costs nothing and can help the client feel better. Remember that complaints can help you to improve your service in future.

有些投诉是合理的,有些投诉可能根本就不是你的错。但是最好还是向客人道歉并采取措施。在服务行业中,客人永远是对的(即使他/她是错的)。道歉不用你付出任何代价,并且能够让客人感觉舒服一点。记住:投诉有助于你改善今后的服务。

技能实训 30　处理投诉
Dealing with Complaints

Section A
Basic Knowledge for Position 岗位基础知识

I. Word Stock 词库

complaint	投诉
criticism	批评
justified	公平的，公正的
constructive	建设性的
rude	粗鲁的
abusive	侮辱的
sympathy	同情
reasonable	合理的
patient	有耐心的
explanation	解释
satisfied	满意的
dissatisfied	不满意
receptionist	接待员
waitress	女服务员
housekeeper	客房主管
general manager	总经理
restaurant manager	餐厅经理
hotel regulation	饭店规定
misunderstanding	误解
promise	答应，承诺
request	请求，要求
account	账目
free of charge	免费
overcharge	过度收费，多收费
solve the problem	解决问题

make compensation for	补偿，赔偿
responsible	负责任
deposit	寄存，存放
describe	描述，描写

Ⅱ. Pronunciation 语音训练

1. My steak is overcooked.
   我的牛排太老了。
2. The heating in my room isn't working. It's as hot as hell up there.
   房间的空调好像出了问题，房间里热得像地狱一样。
3. The wine waiter was very rude to me.
   酒水服务员对我很无礼。
4. You forgot to wake me up at 6 a.m. Now I've missed my train.
   你忘了在6点钟叫醒我，我误了火车。
5. There's no hot water in my room.
   我的房间没有热水。
6. Did you have this room checked before we moved in? There is no toilet paper in the bathroom and the toilet doesn't flush properly.
   我们住进来之前你们检查过房间吗？卫生间里没有卫生纸，马桶无法正常冲水。
7. Could you speed up your switchboard a bit, please? I booked a call to Tokyo 20 minutes ago and I haven't had a reply yet.
   你们能不能让总机速度快一点？我20分钟前就预订了打往东京的电话，但现在还没有回应。
8. The service is too slow. When can we have our soup?
   服务太慢了，你们什么时候才能上我们点的汤？
9. I'm terribly sorry about that, sir.
   很抱歉，先生。
10. I'm really very sorry about this, madam.
    女士，我真的很抱歉。
11. I'll do it right away, sir.
    先生，我现在马上做。
12. I'll see to it right away, madam.
    女士，我马上处理这件事。
13. I'll send a repairman to your room immediately, Mr. Brown.
    布朗先生，我马上派一个维修人员到您的房间。
14. I'll make sure it won't happen again.
    我保证这样的事情不会再发生。

Section B

Service Procedure 服务流程

1. Greeting the guest.
   向客人打招呼。
2. Ask what's the matter.
   询问出了什么问题。
3. Listen patiently.
   耐心倾听。
4. Make an apology.
   表达歉意。
5. Ensure the guest to solve the problem.
   向客人保证解决问题。
6. Extend good wishes to the guest.
   向客人送上美好的祝愿。

Ⅰ. Service Performance 服务演练

M = Manager（经理）　　G= Guest（客人）

M：Good afternoon, madam. Did you want to see me?
　　下午好，女士。您要见我吗？

G：Yes, I did. I'm not satisfied.
　　是的。我很不满意。

M：What's wrong? Perhaps you'd like to tell me what the problem is.
　　怎么了？也许您愿意告诉我发生了什么事情。

G：It's my fish. Look, there is a hair in it. But when I told your waiter about it, he didn't take any notice.
　　这是我点的鱼。你看，我的这盘鱼里有一根头发。但当我告诉服务员的时候，他根本就不当回事。

M：I'm very sorry about it, madam. I'm sure the waiter didn't mean to be rude. Perhaps he didn't understand you correctly. In addition, some of our staff are still going through the training. I know he should change it for you, but …

女士，对此我表示非常抱歉。我可以肯定服务员不是故意表现得很无礼，也许他没理解您的意思。另外，我们的一些服务员还在接受培训。我知道他是想帮您换一盘的，但是……

G：Well, why didn't he?

哦，那为什么他没那么做呢？

M：There must be some misunderstanding, madam. I do apologize for it. I'll change your fish right away.

肯定是误会了，女士。我对此表示道歉。我马上就给您换。

G：Good. That's better. And another thing is this wine. I think it is corked.

好的。这还差不多。还有一件事就是这瓶酒，我认为它有一股怪味。

M：Are you sure, madam? The Claret has been very nice.

真的吗？女士。这瓶红葡萄酒味道非常好的。

G：Here, taste it yourself.

那你自己尝尝吧。

(Having tasted a bit.)（尝了一点点。）

M：No, there doesn't seem to be anything wrong with it. Maybe it is a bit bitter for you. I'd recommend you to try the old Tom Gin next time, madam.

没有啊，这酒一点怪味都没有。也许对您来说会有点苦。女士，我推荐您下次可以尝试一下老汤姆金酒。

G：OK, perhaps I will. Aha, here comes the fish. Shall I pay for that one?

好的，也许吧。哦，鱼来了。这盘鱼我需要付钱吗？

M：Of course not. It's all free of charge. Please take your time and enjoy your meal.

当然不需要，是免费的。请慢慢品尝。

G：Thank you.

谢谢。

M：It's my pleasure. And I'm always at your service.

别客气。愿意随时为您服务。

Ⅱ. Position Practice 岗位实训

★ Practice the following ten steps when dealing with complaints. （处理客人投诉时，请注意以下十个步骤。）

1. Listen attentively.
   专心听。

2. Keep calm.
   保持冷静。

3. Sympathize the guest.
   同情客人。

4. Protect guest's self-esteem.
   保护客人的自尊。

5. Value the guest.
   重视客人。

6. Take notes of the guest's demands.
   记下客人的要求。

7. Keep the guest informed of the measures or actions you intend to take.
   告知客人酒店要采取的措施。

8. Make sure when measures will be carried out.
   确认这些措施何时实施。

9. Supervise the remedies and corrections.
   监督补救或改正措施的实施。

10. Feedback information.
    反馈信息。

★ Express your willingness to help the guest. （表达你乐意帮助客人。）

1. Thank you for telling us about it, sir. I'll look into the matter at once.
   感谢您为我们提供这些情况，我立即调查这件事。

2. I'll tell the person in charge and ask him to take care of the problem.
   我会告诉负责人，让他来处理这件事。

3. Please calm down, sir. I'll try to help you.
   先生，请您冷静。我会尽力帮助您。

4. Please relax, madam. I will take care of it at your request.
   请放心，女士。我将按您的要求办。

Ⅲ. Listening Practice 听力实训

★ A. Listen to the following passage about complaints and fill in the missing information.

Hotel guest complaints frequently _____ the cleanliness of the bed or bathroom, but there may be complaints about any aspect of the guest's _____ _____. To deal with a guest complaint in a hotel, the first step is to _____ the guest's full complaint. When expressing a complaint, the guest may be _____. They need to be fully _____ even if all the relevant details are made known right away. Then ask questions to _____ what actions will be taken to fix the _____. If a problem cannot be solved, Front Office staff should admit this to the guest _____. _____ is the best method when dealing with guest complaints.

★ B. Complete the following conversation.

Guest: Waitress!
Waitress: Yes? _____?
Guest: Not exactly. _____. I asked for it well-done! And it's rather cold.
Waitress: I do apologize, sir. Would you _____?
Guest: Please.
Waitress: Would you like something else _____?
Guest: Yes, some French fries please. But tell them to hurry.
Waitress: Sure. But the restaurant is very busy today. _____.

Important 特别关注

▲ When dealing with complaints from the guests, it is very important to keep the following four things in your mind: listening, sympathizing, apologizing, and telling the guests what has been done to solve their problems.
在应对客人投诉时，要牢记四点：倾听、同情、道歉和告诉客人你们已经做了哪些努力。

▲ Quickly and properly solving guest's complaints can help your business grow and prosper. Ignoring complaints or dealing with them in a dishonest manner can result in loss of business or even lawsuits.
快速、合理地处理投诉有助于生意兴隆，忽视或者用不诚实的手段处理投诉会带来生意上的损失甚至被起诉。

Section C

Case and Development 案例与创新

Case 案例

The guest complained to you:
The chambermaid burst into his room and woke him up this morning.
The chambermaid didn't come back to make up his room till the afternoon.
The chambermaid didn't clean the bathroom properly.

Development 创新

• Is it possible and necessary for a department head to fulfill all the requests of guests? If not, what is to be done?

• When you or your staff members are wronged by an unhappy guest, what should you do?

• Shall we encourage guests' complaints? Why or why not?

技能实训 31　刁钻客人 Difficult Guests

听力音频

Section A

Basic Knowledge for Position 岗位基础知识

Ⅰ. Word Stock 词库

critical	挑剔的
awkward	难处理的；难对付的；令人尴尬的
abusive	辱骂人的，滥用的
compliment	称赞；恭维
commendation	赞扬；推荐
criticism	批评
justified	公正的
constructive	建设性的；积极的
reasonable	合理的
argument	争吵
perspective	角度
fastidious	难以取悦的；吹毛求疵的；挑剔的
undesirable	不受欢迎的；令人不快的
understanding	理解；谅解；领悟
sympathy	同情

Ⅱ. Pronunciation 语音训练

1. There seems to be something strange in my soup.
   我的汤有怪味。
2. I've been waiting a very long time for someone to bring me my bill.
   我等我的账单已经等了很长时间了。
3. I left my Walkman in my room while I was out. When I returned it was lying on the floor broken.
   我出去的时候把我的随身听放在房间里。当我回来的时候随身听在地板上，而且摔坏了。
4. Someone came to my room this morning and tried to sell me something.
   今天早上有人来我的房间推销产品。

5. You recommended the sightseeing tour to me but it was a waste of time.
   你给我介绍的城市观光简直是浪费时间。

6. I'm sure the waiter didn't mean to be rude. Perhaps he didn't understand you correctly.
   我确信服务员不想如此无礼,他可能没有准确理解您的意思。

7. I'm sorry, sir. There must be some misunderstanding.
   很抱歉,先生,一定有误会。

8. Please relax, madam. I'll take care of it at your request.
   请放松,女士。我们会按照您的要求照办的。

9. I'll speak to the person in charge and ask him to take care of the problem.
   我会跟负责的人说,叫他来处理这个问题。

10. Just a moment, sir. I'll get the manager.
    请稍等,先生,我去叫经理。

11. Excuse me, but I should say it's against our hotel's regulations.
    请原谅,但我得说这违反了我们酒店的规定。

12. Please, sir. If you calm yourself, I'll try to help you.
    先生,请冷静,我将尽量帮您。

13. We'll try our best. But I cannot guarantee anything.
    我们将尽力而为,但我无法保证什么。

Section B

Service Procedure 服务流程

1. Greetings.
   问候。

2. Ask what's the matter.
   询问出了什么问题。

3. Listen patiently.
   耐心倾听。

4. Make an apology.
   表达歉意。

5. Deal with the complaints.
   处理投诉。

6. Make good wishes to the guest.
   表达良好祝愿。

I. Service Performance 服务演练

H＝Housekeeper（客房部主管）　　G＝Guest（客人）

H：Housekeeping. May I help you?
　　这里是客房部，需要我帮忙吗？

G：Yes, I'm afraid the room attendant did not properly clean my room.
　　是的。我想服务员没有把我房间打扫干净。

H：I'm awfully sorry, madam.
　　对不起，女士。

G：There is dust on the chest of wardrobe.
　　衣柜上都是灰。

H：Please let me apologize for this. I will send a room attendant to dust it right away.
　　对此我表示道歉。我会立刻派一个客房服务员来把它擦干净。

G：And there's another problem. The window of my bedroom don't close properly.
　　还有一个问题。我卧室的窗户关不严。

H：I will send a repairman to fix it right away. Are there any other problems, madam?
　　我马上叫一个维修工来修理。女士，还有其他问题吗？

G：Yes, I was woken up by the noise from the top floor at 7:30 this morning. What's wrong?
　　是的，今天早上 7:30 我就被顶层的噪声吵醒了。这是怎么回事？

H：I will look into this matter myself. We will make sure that this won't happen again.
　　我会亲自去调查这件事。我们会确保此类事情不会再发生。

G：That's very kind of you.
　　谢谢。

H：Please, madam, don't hesitate to contact us again if you have any further problems.
　　女士，如果还有其他问题，请直接提出来。

G：Well, I think I've complained enough today.
　　哦，我想我今天说得够多了。

H：You have the right to complain, madam. We want to make your stay as comfortable as possible. By the way, both the repairman and the room attendant will be right up.
　　女士，这是应该的。我们希望您在这里住得舒服。顺便告诉您，修理工和客房服务员马上就到。

G：Very well. Thank you very much.

好的。非常感谢。

H：Thank you for calling, madam.
感谢您给我们打电话，女士。

Ⅱ. Position Practice 岗位实训

★ Guests can be difficult in three ways.（三种类型的刁钻客人）

1. The distracted guest brings all his problems with him.
   心烦意乱的客人带来他所有的问题。
2. The disappointed guest arrives with certain expectation.
   失望的客人带着一定的期待。
3. The disruptive guest calls for emergency action.
   对捣乱的客人需要采取紧急措施。

★ Suggestions for dealing with difficult guests.（与刁钻客人打交道的一些建议）

1. If the guest's problem is a result of an error on hotel's side, it's best to admit it and apologize.
   如果客人的问题是酒店的失误造成的，最好承认并道歉。
2. Please make a relevant effort to solve the problem and let the guest have as much feedback as possible.
   要做出相应的努力来解决问题，并给客人尽可能多的反馈。
3. Remember to deal with the guest's feelings. Avoid saying things like："I understand how you feel…" It's better to say："This must be frustrating."
   记得照顾客人的感受，避免说类似"我理解你的感受……"这样的话，最好说"这一定很恼人"。
4. Everybody wants to make a contribution. So involve the guest in the solution whenever possible. Ask question like："What would you suggest?"
   每个人都需要参与感。所以，如果有可能，就请你的客人参与问题的解决，问他类似"您有什么建议？"这样的问题。
5. Show your guest some genuine care.
   向客人表达你真诚的关心。

Ⅲ. Listening Practice 听力实训

★ A. Listen to the following passage about difficult guests and fill in the missing information.

As a new hotel manager, you have to _____ the unexpected. And among the many challenges faced by all hotel managers is the overly _____. Sometimes, it's a _____ with very specific and unusual demands. There are also the party-hearty musicians who leave your _____ a total mess. When you encounter a difficult guest, keep in mind that such guests may have had a _____ while traveling. They may have missed a _____, had their luggage damaged or misplaced, or simply had a bad day or _____. They may have arrived at your hotel with all this negative feelings already in their heads and just need someone or something to vent their frustrations upon. On the other hand, their problem may stem from _____ in your hotel. Either way, here are some _____ to help you deal with it: hear and understand; don't go on defensive; keep a _____ tone and don't over promise.

★ B. Complete the following conversation.

Receptionist: Good afternoon, madam. May I help you?
Guest: Yes. I settled my account this morning, but _____.
Receptionist: May I have your room number please?
Guest: 1316.
Receptionist: 1316. And _____?
Guest: The laundry charge is too high. I only used the laundry service once. It can't be 300 yuan. It's impossible.
Receptionist: Just a minute, madam. _____. Thank you for waiting. According to our records, you used the laundry service three times. I have our copies of your laundry bills here. _____?
Guest: Yes. I think there must be a mistake. I only used the laundry service once.
Receptionist: Here are your laundry slips, madam. _____?
Guest: No, only one slip is mine.
Receptionist: _____.
Guest: Oh, my god, it's my husband's signature.
Receptionist: I see.
Guest: I'm sorry for the trouble.
Receptionist: It doesn't matter. Have a good day.

Important 特别关注

▲ If you promised the guest that you would do something about his problem, do what you promise. Otherwise it will lead your hotel to loads of damage.
如果你答应了客人你将做点什么来解决问题，你就要遵守诺言。言而无信会给酒店带来巨大的损失。

▲ Guests don't start out being difficult. If they are paid attention to early on and their matters are properly handled in the beginning, chances are that you can turn things around.

客人并非一开始就是难缠的。如果他们能够早点被关注或者问题一开始就得到恰当的处理，你就可以扭转局面。

Section C

Case and Development 案例与创新

Case 案例

You are hard to please. You are dissatisfied because:

You ordered breakfast in your room and they brought you coffee instead of tea.

The coffee was cold.

And you ordered it for 8 a.m. but they brought it at 7:30.

Last night the fire alarm rang at midnight. It was a false alarm.

The fire escape route was locked.

You had to stand outside the hotel in your pajamas for half an hour till you were allowed back in.

Nobody apologized for this at the time.

Development 创新

• Have you had any similar experiences of difficult clients? Tell each other what happened and how you dealt with them.

• What kinds of guests do you find most difficult to deal with?

• How do you understand the saying: "Customers are always right"?

实训模块九

其他服务
Other Services

This module focuses on lost and found, deposit service and tourism information introduction as well. The room attendant should check the room thoroughly after the guest checks out. If the guest leaves his belongings in the room, the room attendant should inform the front desk immediately. If the guest has already left the hotel, the room attendant should record the information in the lost and found form with details including the room number, the guest's name, item name and the finder's name. Generally, the belongings can be kept up to one year.

本模块重点学习失物招领、寄存服务和旅游信息介绍。客人离店后,服务员要仔细检查客房。若发现有客人遗留物品,服务员应立即通知前台。若此时客人已离去,服务员应将客人的遗留物品记录于《失物招领表》上,并注明房号、客人的姓名、物品名称、拾物者的姓名。失物一般保存一年。

技能实训 32　失物招领服务 Lost and Found

Section A

Basic Knowledge for Position 岗位基础知识

Ⅰ. Word Stock 词库

lost and found	失物招领处
problem	麻烦，问题
purse	钱包（女用）
wallet	钱包（男用）
check	检查
unusual	不寻常的
common/normal	正常的
ordinary	普通的
direction	方向
visible	看得见的
worried	着急的
concerned	关心的
anxious	焦虑的
electronic dictionary	电子词典
description	描述
portable	手提的
contact	联系
make an appointment	预约
in advance	提前
lost property	失物

Ⅱ. Pronunciation 语音训练

1. Today is a terrible day. I have just lost my mobile phone. All my contacts are in it. It is really important to me.
   今天真不走运，我刚刚丢了手机。我的所有的通讯录都在里面，它对我太重要了。

2. What is the brand of your phone? And what's the color?
   您的手机是什么牌子的？什么颜色？

3. Can you give us a detailed description of your lost watch?
   您能够详细给我们描述一下您丢失的手表吗?
4. When did you last use your laptop computer?
   您最后一次使用您的手提电脑是在什么时候?
5. Would you please fill in the lost property form?
   请您填写一下财产遗失单好吗?
6. Would you please show us your passport?
   请出示您的护照好吗?
7. We will send the room attendant to check now. We will see you at the lost and found.
   我们会让客房服务员立刻查看。我们在失物招领处等您。
8. You are really lucky, our staff found one in the hallway yesterday. I think it belongs to your daughter.
   您真幸运。昨天我们的工作人员在走廊捡到一个。我想是您女儿的。
9. You may find your handbag at the lost and found.
   您也许可以在失物招领处找到您的手袋。
10. They decided to send it to the hotel's lost and found.
    他们决定把它送到酒店的失物招领处去。

Section B

Service Procedure 服务流程

1. Put numbered tags on the items found.
   对拾到的物品进行编号。
2. Ask the guest to fill in the lost property form.
   请客人填写财产遗失单。
3. Keep the record of the lost item.
   保存好丢失物品的记录。
4. Ask the guest to fill in the claim form.
   请客人填写取物单。
5. Ask the guest to show his ID card.
   请客人出示身份证明。
6. Check and return the lost property to the guest.
   核对并归还失物。

Ⅰ. Service Performance 服务演练

A＝Mrs. Brown（布朗太太）　　B＝Mr. Brown（布朗先生）　　S＝Security Department（保安部）

A：Operator, put me through to the security department, please.
　　接线员，请帮我接通保安部。

S：Security department. How can I help you?
　　这里是保安部。我能为您做什么？

A：My husband's gold watch is missing and I need your help.
　　我丈夫的金表不见了，我需要你的帮助。

S：Just take it easy. I'll be in your room in a minute. What's your name and room number, please?
　　别着急。我马上去您的房间。您能告诉我您的姓名和房号吗？

A：Mrs. Brown, room 802.
　　我是 802 房间的布朗太太。

(A few minutes later, there is a knock at the door. Mr. Brown opens the door.)
（过了一会儿，敲门声响起。布朗先生打开了门。）

S：How do you do, Mr. and Mrs. Brown.
　　布朗先生，布朗太太，你们好！

B：How do you do, officer. Please come in and take a seat.
　　你好，先生。请进，请坐。

S：Are you sure that your watch isn't still somewhere in your room?
　　您确定您的手表不在房间里吗？

B：Yes. I've looked everywhere in my room and I can't find it.
　　是的。我找遍了整个房间，但找不到。

S：When and where did you last see it?
　　您最后一次看到它是在什么时候？在哪里看见的？

B：Let me see … Last night on the dresser. I took it off before I went for a shower and forgot to put it back this morning.
　　让我想想……是昨晚在梳妆台上。我洗澡前把它摘下来的，今天早上忘了戴上它。

S：Are you sure you didn't wear it this morning?
　　您确定您今天早上没戴吗？

B：Yes, I'm sure.
　　是的，我肯定。

S：Did you remember to lock your door before you left then?
　　您记得在你们离开房间的时候把门锁好了吗？

B：Yes, I think I did.
　　是的，我想是的。

S: Has anyone been to your room since then?
之前有人来过你们的房间吗？

B: Er ... the room attendant came with two bottles of water and newspaper.
嗯……客房服务员来过，拿来了两瓶水和一份报纸。

A: And the laundryman came to collect our laundry.
洗衣房服务员来拿过我们要洗的衣服。

B: (Writing all the details down) Don't worry about that, Mr. and Mrs. Brown. We will try our best to get it back for you.
（写下所有的细节）别担心，布朗先生和布朗太太。我们将尽力为您找到。

[There is a knock at the door. Mr. Brown opens the door and a laundryman (L) comes in with a gold watch in his hand.]
（敲门声响起。布朗先生打开了门，洗衣房服务员手中拿着金表进来了。）

L: Is this yours, Mr. Brown? I found it in the laundry.
布朗先生，这是您的吗？我在您要洗的衣服里找到的。

B: Yes, it is mine.
是的，是我的。

A: You are always so careless.
你总是不小心。

B: I am sorry for that. I'll be careful next time.
不好意思。我下次一定小心。

S: It's all right.
没关系。

A: (To the laundryman) Thank you very much.
（对洗衣房服务员）非常感谢你。

L: You are welcome.
别客气。

Ⅱ. Position Practice 岗位实训

★ Show sympathy for the guest. （对客人表示同情）

1. Don't worry, sir/madam, we'll check to it immediately.
   先生/女士，请不要担心，我们会立刻为您查询。

2. I am really sorry to hear this, but we will try to help you with it.
   很抱歉听到这个消息，但我们会尽力帮助您。

★ Ask for the details of the item. （询问丢失物品的信息）

1. What is the brand of your watch/phone/wallet?
   您的手表/手机/钱包是什么牌子的？

2. What color is it?
   它是什么颜色的？

3. Is it brand new?
   它是崭新的吗？

★ Respond to the guests' request. （回复客人的请求）
   1. We will see to it immediately.
      我们立刻处理此事。
   2. I am sorry, it has not been found yet.
      很抱歉，还没有找到。

★ Ask for the guest's personal information. （询问客人的个人信息）
   1. May I have your name/room number/address?
      能留下您的姓名/房号/地址吗？
   2. Could you show me your ID card?
      能否出示您的身份证？
   3. Would you mind leaving your name/address here?
      可否留下您的姓名/住址？

★ Ask the guest to fill out the relevant forms. （要求客人填写相关表格）
   1. Could you fill in the lost property form?
      您能填写一下财产遗失单吗？
   2. Would you mind filling in the claim form?
      请您填写一下取物单。

Ⅲ. Listening Practice 听力实训

★ A. Listen to the following passage about lost and found and fill in the missing information.

What's the most commonly _____ of guests in hotel rooms? It's not the _____ peanuts from the _____. Hotel guests are walking away from some of their most private possessions when they _____ of hotels, but just how personal are the items? _____ a check of 31 UK hotels' lost property departments, you may _____ about the _____ objects left behind in hotel rooms by their guests. Among the items housekeeping has picked up in hotel rooms, _____ chargers and underwear top the list of most commonly left behind items, amongst the most unusual items guests forgot to take with them when they checked out were a _____, wigs, musical instruments and _____. We want to know: What items have you left behind in hotel rooms? Did you get them back?

★ B. Complete the following conversation.

Attendant: You look worried, sir. _____?
Guest: I've lost my key.

Attendant: Oh, perhaps _____.
Guest: Thanks. It must be here somewhere.
Attendant: _____?
Guest: Yes. It's not there.
Attendant: Have you checked in your bag?
Guest: Hold on, let me see... No, it's not there.
Attendant: Well, _____?
Guest: It wouldn't be there, would it? I'll check anyway? Nope!
Attendant: _____?
Guest: Under my desk?
Attendant: Did you look on the floor?
Guest: On the floor? Wait a moment... Ah ha! I've got it. Thanks.
Attendant: You're welcome.

Important 特别关注

▲ When reporting lost property, please provide a detailed description. Due to the large number of enquiries, please include any unique characteristics instead of giving a generic description.
报告失物时,请提供一份详细的描述。因为有大量的失物查询,所以要提供有特征的描述而不是通用的描述。

▲ If you are claiming property for another person, his written authorisation will be required. Personal identification will be required in cases of property collection.
如果您为他人领取财物,必须要有那人的书面授权。在领取财物时也必须提供个人的身份证明。

Section C

Case and Development 案例与创新

Case 案例

Suppose that the receptionist at the lost and found gets a phone call from Mr. Brown in the morning. He has checked out, but he has left his laptop computer in the room. The room attendant will take the laptop computer to the lost and found. Mr. Brown will come to claim it.

Development 创新

• What information should be filled in the lost and found form?

• If the guest makes a mistake about what he lost, what will you do if you are a hotel attendant?

• What are the most important points you should make sure when the guest comes to claim the lost property?

技能实训 33　寄存服务 Deposit Service

听力音频

Section A

Basic Knowledge for Position 岗位基础知识

I. Word Stock 词库

switch	开关
master key	万能钥匙
wardrobe	衣柜，衣橱
slot	插槽
nightstand	床头柜
socket	插座
indicate	显示，暗示
password	密码
arbitrarily	任意地
decode	解密
luggage application form	行李寄存单

II. Pronunciation 语音训练

1. Excuse me. I will check out later at noon. I wonder whether I could leave my luggage here after I check out.
   你好，我中午要退房。我想问一下退房后能否在这里寄存行李？

2. We do provide deposit service. When will you collect them?
   我们有寄存服务。您想什么时候提行李？

3. We will collect your luggage at 11 a.m. Would you come to the service desk then to get your luggage tag?
   我们会在11点钟为您提取行李。然后请您来服务台领行李标签好吗？

4. I would like to use a safety deposit box. Will it fit the size of this box?
   我想使用一个保险箱。这个东西放得下吗？

5. Could you fill out this form and sign at the bottom, please?
   请您填写这份表格并在下面签字。

6. Please put your items in this bag, and we will seal it.
   请您把东西放在这个袋子里，我们会密封它。

7. If you would like to use the items during the period of storage, please come here in person with the tag. After confirming your signature, we will open the safe.
   如果在寄存期间您要领取物品，请您亲自过来并出示取物牌。我们核对签名后会为您打开保险箱。

Section B

Service Procedure 服务流程

1. Greeting.
   问候。

2. Ask the guest to fill in the luggage application form.
   请客人填写行李寄存单。

3. Explain the cost of the service and charge the guest.
   解释收费标准并收费。

4. Give the guest a tag for claiming.
   给客人取物牌。

5. Extend good wishes to the guest.
   向客人表达良好的祝愿。

Ⅰ. Service Performance 服务演练

A = Attendant（服务生）　　G = Guest（客人）

A：Good morning, sir. What can I do for you?
先生，早上好。我能为您做什么？

G：Yes. Can you show me how to use the safe in my room? I'll go to Beijing on business for two days and I want to keep some documents in it while I'm away.
是的。你能告诉我房间里的保险箱怎么使用吗？我将去北京出差两天。我想在离开的时候把文件放在保险箱里。

A：Certainly, sir. If you want to use the safe, please go to the service center first and fill out a signature card, then the clerk there will give you an activation pin.

当然可以，先生。如果您想使用保险箱，请先到服务中心填一张签名卡，然后那里的服务员会给您一根激活销。

G：Activation pin? What's the use of it?

激活销？它有什么用处？

A：Once you get the pin, please plug in and open the door of the safe, insert the pin, then "OPEN" will be shown on the door.

您拿到激活销后，请接通保险箱的电源、拉开箱门、插入激活销，这时门上会显示"开锁"。

G：How do I lock the safe?

那我怎么锁上保险箱呢？

A：After "OPEN" is shown, you must input a six-digit cipher code and the safe will be locked when closed.

当门上显示"开锁"时，你必须输入一个六位数的密码。当关上门时，保险箱就被锁上了。

G：How do I open it when I come back?

当我回来后，我如何打开保险箱呢？

A：Just input the password and open the safe after it is decoded. If you keep the code unchanged, the safe will be locked automatically when the door is closed.

您只要输入密码，待开锁后，再拉开箱门。如果您不改密码，则关上门便会自动上锁。

G：Can other people open it?

其他人能打开它吗？

A：Unless they know the code. The safe will not unlock if you input the wrong code, and it will show "ERROR".

除非他们知道密码。如果您输入错误的密码，保险箱是打不开的，门上将会显示"错误"的字样。

G：Well, it's very safe.

好的，非常安全。

A：I think so. But be sure not to forget the code you set. Otherwise, you have to contact the service center and ask the clerk to open it for you.

是的。但是记住别忘了您设置的密码，否则的话，您就必须联系服务中心，请工作人员帮您开保险箱了。

G：Oh, I see. Thank you very much indeed.

哦，我明白了。非常感谢。

A：It's my pleasure. One more thing, if you stop using the safe, please remove the activation pin and return it to the service center.
很高兴为您服务。还有一件事，如果您不用保险箱了，请拿走激活销并还给服务中心。

G：Sure. Thank you again. Goodbye.
当然。再次感谢。再见。

A：Goodbye, sir. Wish you a pleasant journey.
再见，先生。希望您旅途愉快。

Ⅱ. Position Practice 岗位实训

★ When the guest comes to the desk, you can greet him/her by saying the following. （当客人来到服务台时，你可以用如下表达问候客人）

1. May I help you?
   能为您效劳吗？

2. Good morning/afternoon, would you like to deposit or collect something?
   早上好/下午好，您要存取什么吗？

★ If the guest needs a safety deposit box to store valuables, remind the guest the following. （如果客人需要保险箱寄存贵重物品，提醒客人如下事项）

1. Keep the key carefully.
   小心保存钥匙。

2. Fill out the application form.
   填写申请表。

3. Sign his/her name.
   签名。

4. Keep the tag in a safe place.
   保存好取物牌。

★ Inform the guest of the price with the following expressions. （用下列表达告知客人收费标准）

1. The service costs you ×× yuan per bag per day.
   行李寄存需要支付每件每天××元。

2. The safety deposit box service is free.
   保险箱寄存服务是免费的。

实训模块九 其他服务 Other Services

Ⅲ. Listening Practice 听力实训

★ A. Listen to the following passage about deposit service and fill in the missing information.

Small hotels don't usually have luggage _____ although they will usually _____ for people _____ whose room isn't _____ or for people _____ who need to leave bags until a _____ . Most hotel luggage storage spaces are just _____ to hold bags for a few hours as people _____ . So, if the answer is "we don't have enough room", that's probably _____ . If you just want to _____ your bags and _____ them when you return and move on _____ additional nights stay, it all depends on the space of the hotel _____ or not.

★ B. Complete the following conversation.

Receptionist: Here is your bill, madam. _____ yuan. Please _____ .

Guest: Sure. My flight is 11 p.m. _____ ?

Receptionist: Certainly, madam. Is there anything _____ in your bag?

Guest: No, there isn't.

Receptionist: We'll keep it for you. _____ .

Guest: Thank you. When does the cloakroom close?

Receptionist: This cloakroom is _____ .

Guest: Oh, dear! I won't be back until about 8:30 tonight. Where can I pick up my bag?

Receptionist: We will transfer your bag to _____ . You may collect it there, ma'am.

Guest: I see. Thanks a lot.

Receptionist: You're welcome.

Important 特别关注

▲ When a guest wants to deposit some valuables, confirm his identification. If he is a in-house guest, the service can be provided.
存物品时，要确认客人的身份。如是住店客人，可以提供此项服务。

▲ Ask the guest to show his room card and confirm his room number. Finally verify guest's registered name in the computer.

请客人出示房卡，确认他的房号，核对电脑系统中客人的登记姓名。

▲ When the guest wants to collect his belongings, check his identification.

取寄存物时，应验证客人的身份。

Section C

Case and Development 案例与创新

Case 案例

A guest wants to store his luggage in the hotel after checking out, for he will be on a trip for several days. He will check out at 11：30 this morning, and will claim his luggage a week later. The charge for the service is 5 yuan per bag per day.

Development 创新

- Who should be responsible for the valuables a guest lost in his room?
- If the guest forgets his password of the safety box in his room, what can you do to help him?
- How can you help the guest if he has lost the claim tag?

技能实训 34　介绍旅游信息
Tourism Information

听力音频

Section A

Basic Knowledge for Position 岗位基础知识

Ⅰ. Word Stock 词库

city tour	城市观光
sightseeing	观光
scenic spot	景点
tourist attraction	旅游景点
public transport	公共交通
art gallery	艺术馆
historical museum	历史博物馆
theme park	主题公园
castle	城堡
monument	纪念碑
fascinating	引人入胜的
enjoyable	有趣的
unusual	不寻常的
charming	迷人的
impressive	留下深刻印象的
unforgettable	难忘的
exhausting	累人的
rewarding/worthwhile	值得做的
The Palace Museum	故宫博物院
The Summer Palace	颐和园
The Great Wall	长城
The West Lake	西湖
National Stadium（"Bird's Nest"）	国家体育场（"鸟巢"）

Ⅱ. Pronunciation 语音训练

1. I have just arrived here. I know little about Hangzhou. Could you tell me some

places to visit?
我今天刚到，还不熟悉杭州这座城市。你能给我介绍一些值得游览的地方吗？

2. I suggest you first visit the West Lake where there are many famous and fantastic places to see, such as Melting Snow at Broken Bridge and Three Pools Mirroring the Moon.
我建议您先去西湖游览，那里有很多著名的和非常迷人的景点，比如断桥残雪和三潭印月。

3. If you are interested in the modern side of the city, you could have a look at the central business districts and do some pleasant shopping.
如果您对这座城市现代化的一面感兴趣，可以看看中央商务区一带，并体验购物乐趣。

4. Why don't you take a free traveling brochure here? It can give you a lot of useful information, including restaurant lists.
您从这里取一份免费的旅游指南吧，里面有很多有用的信息，还有餐馆名录。

5. I was told that there is a famous temple in the city center. Could you tell me where it is?
别人告诉我在市中心有一座非常著名的寺庙，你能告诉我在哪吗？

Section B

Service Procedure 服务流程

1. Greetings.
   问候。
2. Ask whether a guest needs help.
   询问客人是否需要帮助。
3. Introduce some famous scenic spots.
   介绍一些著名的旅游景点。
4. Arrange tour or introduce means of transportation.
   安排旅游或介绍出行方式。
5. Extend good wishes to the guest.
   表达良好祝愿。

Ⅰ. Service Performance 服务演练

R＝Reservationist（预订人员）　　A＝Mr. Brown（布朗先生）　　B＝Mrs. Brown（布朗太太）

R：Good morning!
　　早上好！

B：Good morning! Today we have a whole day for sightseeing, could you tell us some famous scenic spots in Hangzhou?
　　早上好！我们今天有一整天的时间可以游览一下，你能给我们推荐一些杭州著名的景点吗？

R：Is this your first time to Hangzhou?
　　这是你们第一次来杭州吗？

B：No, it's my second time here but last time I was on business, so I didn't go to any places.
　　不，这是我第二次来了。但上一次我是来出差的，所以哪里都没有去。

R：I'm very pleased to suggest that you go to visit the West Lake and Lingyin Temple. They are the most famous places in Hangzhou.
　　我非常高兴为你们推荐西湖和灵隐寺。它们是杭州最著名的景点。

A：Why are they so famous?
　　为什么它们如此著名？

R：Because the West Lake is the symbol of Hangzhou and those who came to Hangzhou but didn't go to the West Lake are considered not having been here. The lotuses in the West Lake are very beautiful too.
　　因为西湖是杭州的象征。来了杭州而没有游览西湖的人被认为是没有来过杭州。西湖的荷花也非常漂亮。

A：Great, we'll go there and take some photos. What about the temple?
　　很好。我们会去转转然后拍些照片。那灵隐寺呢？

R：Lingyin Temple is the oldest, the biggest and the most famous Buddhist temple in southeast China. It has two halls: the Front Hall and the Great Buddha Hall.
　　灵隐寺是中国东南部最古老的、最大的和最著名的佛教寺院。它有两个主要的大殿：天王殿和大雄宝殿。

B：Both places sound worth visiting. By the way, can you show us the way to both places?
　　听起来两个地方都值得一游。随便问一下，你能告诉我们怎样去这两个地方吗？

R：Sure, walk out of the hotel gate, turn right until the first traffic light, then take No. 315 bus, it'll directly take you to the West Lake, you won't miss it. Then you can take No. 7 bus to Lingyin Temple.
　　当然可以。从酒店大门出去向右转，一直向前走到第一个红绿灯，在那里乘坐

315路公交车，它会载你们直达西湖，你们不会错过的。然后你们可以乘坐7路公交车到灵隐寺。

A and B：That's so kind of you.
你真好。

R：My pleasure, have fun.
很高兴为你们服务。希望你们玩得愉快！

Ⅱ. Position Practice 岗位实训

★ Show the directions to the guest.（向客人指路）

1. You can take No. 5 bus, and then change to bus No. 7 at ××.
   您先坐5路公交车，然后在××站换乘7路公交车。

2. Cross the road, go down three blocks and you will see the gallery.
   穿过这条路，向前走三个街区就能看到美术馆了。

3. Please go straight and then turn right at the traffic light.
   直走，在红绿灯处向右拐。

★ Give some advice about sightseeing.（给予旅游建议）

1. I suggest you go to the West Lake.
   我建议您去西湖。

2. If I were you, I would go to the Palace Museum.
   如果是我，我会去故宫博物院。

3. Why not go to the Great Wall? It's a must for foreigners.
   您为什么不去长城呢？长城对外国游客来说是一个必去的地方。

★ The reason why you suggest the scenic spots.（为什么建议去该景点）

1. It hasn't been destroyed. There are a lot of parks to walk in.
   它未曾受到破坏，有很多公园可以散步。

2. The weather is hot and sunny, you can get everywhere easily by public transport.
   天气很好，阳光灿烂，乘坐公共交通可以轻松抵达各个地方。

3. The beach was beautiful with white sand. What a great place for a relaxing holiday.
   白色的沙滩太美妙了，这里真是一个度假休闲的好地方。

Ⅲ. Listening Practice 听力实训

★ A. Listen to the following passage about tourist information and fill in the missing information.

Most hotels offer ＿＿＿＿＿＿＿＿＿＿＿＿＿＿＿, including visitor attractions, ＿＿＿＿＿＿, sightseeing, tourist tips and ＿＿＿＿＿＿＿＿＿＿＿＿＿＿. They will provide you with _____ to know about the city. You'll find a wealth of information about _____ and _____. Whether you are looking for _____ out, food festival or _____, tourist information center will give you some advice. With listings of the top events and offers, you can _____ in the place where you can _____ of your money. If necessary, buy a _____ about the city, discounts in main tourist attractions and free transportation all around the city will be a _____. Everything is easier with a Tourist Card, and it's the best way to _____ the city highlights.

★ B. Complete the following conversation.

Clerk: Beijing _____, may I help you?

Guest: Yes. This is Mr. Harris from Australia. I'd like to have a city tour in Beijing. Could you give me some suggestions?

Clerk: Sure. _____ and how long do you plan to sightsee in Beijing?

Guest: I'm staying at the Beijing Hotel. I'll be in the city for 2 days.

Clerk: Mr. Harris, your hotel is near Tian'anmen Square. So it _____ if you visit Tian'anmen Square first. Then, in the north of the square is the Palace Museum.

Guest: Palace Museum? Is it a new museum?

Clerk: No, it _____ the Forbidden City.

Guest: I see. Then how long do you think I need to see the two places?

Clerk: Well, you need _____ to see both Tian'anmen Square and the Palace Museum.

Guest: I see. Then what about tomorrow?

Clerk: I'd like to recommend the Summer Palace and Yuanmingyuan.

Guest: What's interesting there?

Clerk: The Summer Palace is famous for its _____, large lake, and green hills dotted with colorful pavilions. Yuanmingyuan has plenty of historic ruins. They _____, not to be missed.

Guest: I see, you are so helpful.

Important 特别关注

▲ When returning to your hotel in the evening, enter through the main entrance of the hotel. Be alert and look around before entering parking lots.
夜晚回到酒店的时候，要走酒店的大门。进入停车场前要保持警觉并环顾四周。

▲ Don't draw attention to yourself by displaying large amount of cash or expensive

jewelry.
不要携带大量现金或贵重珠宝，以免引起别人的关注。

▲ Don't invite strangers to your room.
不要邀请陌生人到你的房间来。

Section C

Case and Development 案例与创新

Case 案例

Because of your professional knowledge and because you know about your own region, the guest often asks you for your advice. Join in with a partner and take turns to play the roles of a guest and a receptionist talking about what the guest could do this weekend according to weather conditions.

Development 创新

- What are the most important reasons for people to go for travelling?
- Why are visitors sometimes disappointed when they visit your region? What might discourage them from coming again?
- What is your own idea of an ideal holiday destination?

实训模块九 其他服务 Other Services

技能实训 35　托婴服务 Babysitting Service

听力音频

Section A

Basic Knowledge for Position 岗位基础知识

Ⅰ. Word Stock 词库

childcare	照看孩子
regulation	规定
babysitter	临时保姆
day care	日间护理，日间托儿所
experienced	有经验的
professional	专业的
qualified	合格的
attitude	态度
reliability	可靠性
minimum	最少的，最低的
confirmation	确认
emergency	紧急情况，突发事件
newborn	新出生的（adj.）/新生儿（n.）
entertain	娱乐
outgoing	外向的
contact	联系
feedback	反馈

Ⅱ. Pronunciation 语音训练

1. I'd like to go out this evening. How can I find someone to look after my baby?
   我晚上要出去。我如何才能找到人来照看我的孩子？

2. We need someone to look after our baby. Is such service available here?
   我们需要有人照看小孩。这里有这项服务吗？

3. Yes. We have qualified babysitters.
   是的。我们有合格的临时保姆。

4. They are all well-educated and reliable.
   他们接受过良好的教育，非常可靠。

5. The babysitters are experienced and professional.
   临时保姆们很有经验，也很专业。

6. If you need the service, here is a confirmation form for you to fill in.
   如果您需要此服务，这里有一份确认表需要您填写。

7. You have to fill in the time of the service, basic information of the baby and your signature in the form.
   您得在表格上写上服务时间、孩子的基本情况，还有您的签名。

8. We will arrange the babysitting service for you soon. Have a good time.
   我们马上给您安排托婴服务。祝您玩得愉快！

Section B

Service Procedure 服务流程

1. Greetings.
   问候。

2. Ask whether the guest needs help.
   询问客人是否需要帮助。

3. Introduce babysitting service.
   介绍托婴服务。

4. Arrange babysitting service.
   安排托婴服务。

5. Good wishes.
   良好祝愿。

I. Service Performance 服务演练

G=Guest（客人）　　A=Room Attendant（客房服务员）

G：Will you please do me a favor?
　　你能帮我个忙吗？

A：Certainly, if I can do it.
　　当然可以，如果我能做到。

G：My husband and I want to go out this evening. So, can you look after the baby for us? It's till midnight.

我的丈夫和我今晚要出去。你能帮我们照看孩子吗？要照看到半夜。

A：I see. But I am afraid that's not possible. It is against our hotel regulations for me to do this service, as attendants, we cannot do our jobs and look after children properly at the same time.

我明白了。我想我可能不行。这违反了酒店的规定，因为酒店服务员不可能在工作时同时照看好孩子。

G：What shall I do, then?

那我该怎么办？

A：Don't worry, madam. Our housekeeping department has a very good babysitting service. There are some part-time babysitters from the room center.

别担心，女士。我们客房部可以提供很好的托婴服务。在房务中心我们有一些兼职保姆。

G：Are they... eh... experienced?

他们……很有经验吗？

A：Yes, madam. They are all well-educated and reliable.

是的，女士。他们都是受过良好教育的值得信赖的人。

G：It's great. Now, could you tell me about the terms of this service?

太好了！现在你能告诉我这项服务的条款吗？

RA：It is 50 yuan an hour, for a minimum of 4 hours.

每小时50元人民币，4小时起步。

G：That's very reasonable.

价格合理。

A：If you ask the housekeeping department, they will give you more details and send a confirmation form for you to sign.

如果您问一下客房部，他们会给您更详细的解释。然后他们会给您一份确认函，您要在上面签字。

G：All right. I'll phone them right away. Thank you.

好的。我现在就打电话。谢谢。

(The guest returns 10 minutes later.)（十分钟后，客人回来了。）

A：Excuse me, madam. May I ask you to sign this confirmation form? Thank you. I hope I haven't disturbed you.

对不起，女士。您可以在确认函上签名吗？谢谢。希望我没有打扰您。

G：Not at all.

没有打扰。

(Signing the form.)（在表上签字。）

Here you are.

给你。

A：Thank you, madam. Good night and have a pleasant evening.

谢谢，女士。晚安，希望您度过一个愉快的夜晚。

Ⅱ. Position Practice 岗位实训

★ Inform the guest of the service charge.（告知客人收费标准）

There is a minimum charge for the babysitting service, you need to pay 50 yuan per hour and the minimum time is two hours.

托婴服务有最低消费，您一个小时需付 50 元，最少服务 2 小时。

★ Ask about the baby's information.（询问幼儿的具体情况）
1. Can I have the baby's name?
   孩子叫什么名字？
2. How old is the baby?
   孩子几岁了？
3. Is she in good condition?
   她的健康状况怎么样？
4. Does he have any healthy problems?
   他有什么健康问题吗？

★ Ask the guest's telephone number.（询问客人的联系电话）
1. May I have your telephone number?
   请告诉我您的电话号码好吗？
2. How can I contact you in emergency?
   紧急情况下如何联系您？

★ Confirm details of the babysitting service.（确认托婴服务的细节）
1. So you need the babysitting service from 8 p.m. to 12 p.m. Is that right?
   您需要托婴服务，从晚上 8 点到晚上 12 点，对吗？
2. You would like to have an active babysitter who is well-educated, is that right?
   您需要一个活泼点的受过良好教育的临时保姆，是吗？

Ⅲ. Listening Practice 听力实训

★ A. Listen to the following passage about babysitting and fill in the missing information.

When traveling with children at ＿＿＿＿＿＿＿, it's impossible to relax and enjoy ＿＿＿＿＿＿＿ (which you're certainly entitled to!) ＿＿＿＿＿＿＿ getting a sitter. If you want to enjoy the spa or a ＿＿＿＿＿＿＿ in a hotel, you can ask babysitting service in the hotel. Quality hotels are very ＿＿＿＿＿＿＿ about the babysitters they recommend, because of the obvious liability issues. Here is how _____ works: the hotels contract out to a babysitting service, which interviews and screens the babysitters. The Concierge _____ the babysitting service of a guest's needs, and the service then finds an _____ sitter. Sitters are paid _____, and a portion of the bill goes back to the service. You should _____ instructions on whether or not the kids are allowed to leave the hotel room.

★ B. Complete the following conversation.

Guest: Excuse me, madam. Could you do me a favor?

Concierge: Yes, _____. What's the matter?

Guest: I've made an appointment with my business partner tonight. I need someone to look after my baby. Is babysitting service available here?

Concierge: Yes, we have _____ babysitters.

Guest: That's good. Could you tell me how much babysitting service is charged?

Concierge: It is 60 yuan per hour, _____.

Guest: That's OK.

Concierge: Do you have _____?

Guest: Yes, my baby is not allowed to leave the hotel room.

Concierge: Sure. The babysitter _____.

Guest: Thank you.

Concierge: If you need the service, please _____.

Guest: OK, I will finish it right away.

Concierge: _____ here, madam?

Guest: Sure. Here you are.

Concierge: Thank you, madam. We will arrange the service soon. Have a good night.

Important 特别关注

▲ Pay close attention to the baby's safety.
密切关注婴儿的安全问题。

▲ Babysitters should be carefully selected, qualified, and professional who are experienced in caring for children from newborn to school age.
要精挑细选合格、专业的临时保姆,能够照看从刚出生到学龄段的孩子。

▲ If the babysitter is not friendly, not confident enough, looks untidy, or if you have any doubts, you'd better not leave the baby to that person.
如果临时保姆不友好、不够自信,看起来不太整洁,或者您有任何怀疑,最好就不要把孩子交给那个人。

Section C

Case and Development 案例与创新

Case 案例

A guest is complaining that her baby was not taken good care of by a babysitter. Make the dialogue.

Development 创新

- If the baby you take care of is not feeling very well, what should you do?
- If the guest doesn't come back on time to bring her baby, what should you do?
- Who shall you inform first when there is an emergency for a baby?

附录一

饭店日常用语

1. Good morning, sir/madam.
   早上好,先生/女士。
2. Good evening, ladies and gentlemen.
   晚上好,女士们先生们。
3. Hello. Glad/Nice to meet you.
   您好,很高兴见到您。
4. How are you?
   您好吗?
5. Fine, Thanks. And you?
   很好,谢谢。您好吗?
6. Welcome to our hotel/restaurant/shop.
   欢迎到我们饭店/餐厅/商店。
7. Thank you for your coming.
   谢谢您的光临。
8. Have a good time!
   祝您过得愉快!
9. Happy New Year!
   新年快乐!
10. Happy Birthday!
    生日快乐!
11. Happy weekend!
    周末愉快!
12. Merry Christmas!
    圣诞快乐!
13. Have a nice holiday!
    假期快乐!

14. Wish you every success! /May you succeed!
    祝您成功！

15. Wish you good luck!
    祝您好运！

16. Wish you a pleasant journey.
    祝您旅途愉快！

17. Wish you a most pleasant stay in our hotel.
    愿您在我们饭店过得愉快。

18. Wish you have a good rest.
    祝您休息得好！

19. Thank you (very much).
    谢谢您（非常感谢）。

20. Thank you for your advice /help.
    感谢您的忠告/帮助。

21. It's very kind of you.
    谢谢，您真客气。

22. You are welcome. /Not at all. /Don't mention it.
    不用谢。

23. It's my pleasure. /With pleasure. /My pleasure.
    非常高兴为您服务。

24. I am at your service.
    乐意为您效劳。

25. Thank you for your staying in our hotel.
    感谢您在我们饭店下榻。

26. I'm sorry.
    很抱歉。

27. Excuse me.
    对不起。

28. I'm sorry. It's my fault.
    很抱歉。那是我的过错。

29. Sorry to have kept you waiting.
    对不起，让您久等了。

30. Sorry to interrupt you.
    对不起，打扰您了。

31. I'm sorry about this.
    我对此表示抱歉。

32. I apologize for this.
    我为此道歉。

33. That's all right.
    没关系。

34. Can/May I help you?
    我能帮您什么吗？

35. Is there anything else I can do for you?
    还有什么能为您效劳的吗？

36. Just a moment, please.
    请稍等一下。

37. May I know your name, please?
    请问尊姓大名？

38. Have a good rest, sir.
    先生，请好好休息。

39. Please sign here, sir.
    先生，请在这签上您的名字。

40. May I see your passport, madam?
    女士，请出示您的护照好吗？

41. What kind of room would you like?
    您要什么样的房型？

42. When for? / For which date?
    什么时候要房间？

43. For how many people?
    一共几个人？

44. How long will you be staying?
    您打算住多久？

45. Could you please spell your name?
    请拼一下您的名字。

46. May I have your telephone number?
    请问您的电话号码？

47. May I introduce myself?
    请允许我自我介绍一下。

48. I'm the receptionist here, welcome to our hotel.
    我是这儿的接待员，欢迎来到我们饭店。

49. That's no problem at all.

没问题。

50. Housekeeping. May I come in?
    客房服务员，我可以进来吗?

51. Leave your laundry in the laundry bag, please.
    请把要洗的东西放在洗衣袋中。

52. I hope I'm not disturbing you.
    我希望没有打扰您。

53. One moment, madam. I'll bring them to you right away.
    等一会儿，女士。我马上送来。

54. I'll send a repairman immediately.
    我马上给您派一个维修工。

55. Is there anything else, sir?
    还有什么事吗，先生?

56. If you need anything else, please call us.
    如果您有什么事请叫我们。

57. It's very kind of you to do so.
    您这样做真是太好了。

58. What's your room number, please?
    请问您的房间号码是多少?

59. May I have a look at your room card?
    我可以看一下您的房卡吗?

60. How do you like this room?
    您觉得这个房间怎么样?

61. When would you like me to do your room, sir?
    您要我什么时间来打扫房间呢，先生?

62. May I offer you turn-down service now?
    我现在可以给您做夜床吗?

63. What time will be convenient for you?
    您什么时候方便?

64. How do you like Chinese food?
    您喜欢中国菜吗?

65. What do you think of our service?
    您对我们的服务有什么意见?

66. Thank you for your suggestions.
    谢谢您给我们提的建议。

67. Sit down, please. Here is the menu.
    请坐，给您菜单。

68. May I take your order, sir?
    先生，您要点菜吗？

69. What would you like to have, coffee or tea?
    您要喝咖啡还是茶？

70. Here is the bill. Please sign it.
    这是您的账单，请签字。

71. I'm afraid it's against the hotel's regulations.
    这是违反饭店规章制度的。

72. In our hotel, we don't accept tips.
    我们饭店是不收小费的。

73. Thank you all the same.
    仍然感谢你。

74. I'm afraid you'll have to compensate for the damage.
    恐怕您得赔偿损失。

75. I'll look into the matter right away.
    我马上去处理这件事情。

76. I assure you it won't happen again.
    我保证此类事情不会再发生。

77. Please don't worry, madam.
    女士，请不要担心。

78. Reservations, may I help you?
    预订部，我能帮您什么吗？

79. Room service, may I come in?
    送餐服务，我可以进来吗？

80. I'm afraid that's not a good idea.
    恐怕那个主意不好。

81. Enjoy you breakfast/lunch/dinner, sir.
    先生，请享用你的早餐/午餐/晚餐。

82. You are through, please go ahead.
    接通了，请讲。

83. A table for four?
    一张四人桌吗？

84. Did you make a reservation?

您预订房间了吗？

85. I'll show you to your room. This way, please.
    我带您去您的房间，这边请。

86. What kind of currency do you have?
    您有什么货币？

87. Please hold the line. I'll put you through in a minute.
    请拿好电话，马上就可以为您接通。

88. I'm sorry the extension is busy just now.
    对不起，电话分机刚才占线。

89. How about the table over there?
    那边的那张餐桌可以吗？

90. I'm sorry. We're rather full tonight.
    对不起，今晚我们这儿客满了。

91. You look very nice in that dress.
    您穿上那件衣服很漂亮。

92. I'm sorry they're sold out.
    对不起，都卖完了。

93. Do you have any special suggestions?
    您有什么特别的建议吗？

94. Hope to see you again.
    希望再次见到您。

95. I'm looking forward to seeing you soon.
    希望很快就能见到您。

附录二

饭店常用告示语

1. Caution! Automatic door.
   注意！自动门。
2. Caution! Don't enter.
   注意！切勿进入。
3. Caution! Hot.
   注意！小心高温。
4. Caution! Wet paint.
   注意！油漆未干。
5. Caution! Wet floor.
   注意！小心地滑。
6. Daily special.
   今日特价。
7. Disposable product.
   一次性产品。
8. Dry Cleaning.
   干洗。
9. Emergency door open.
   应急门开启。
10. Emergency exit.
    紧急通道。
11. Entrance.
    入口。
12. Exit.
    出口。

13. Fire exit.
    消防通道。

14. Flush after use.
    便后请冲水。

15. Fragile.
    易碎品。

16. In business.
    营业中。

17. Keep clear.
    保持通畅。

18. Keep out.
    严禁入内。

19. Mind your head. /Watch your head.
    小心碰头。

20. No admittance except on business.
    非公莫入。

21. No cigarette disposal.
    禁止乱扔烟头。

22. No cycling. /No bicycles.
    禁止骑车。

23. No litter.
    请勿乱扔废弃物。

24. No parking.
    不得停车。

25. No personal checks.
    不接收个人支票。

26. No photography.
    严禁拍照。

27. No spitting.
    禁止随地吐痰。

28. Occupied.
    （厕所）有人。

29. Out of use.
    停用。

30. Please be careful.

请小心。

31. Please mind the step.
    请小心台阶。

32. Please only use in an emergency.
    请仅在紧急情况下使用。

33. Private parking.
    专用车位。

34. Reserved.
    留座。

35. Ring bell for service.
    需要服务，请按铃。

36. Please do not disturb.
    请勿打扰。

37. Room ready for service.
    可以整理房间。

38. Safety exit.
    安全通道。

39. Staff only.
    闲人免进。

40. Toilet for the disabled.
    残障人士专用厕所。

41. Don't litter.
    禁止随便丢弃垃圾。

42. Out of use. Please use the side doors.
    此门停用。请走旁门。

43. To avoid congestion, please do not stop and stay near the stairs.
    楼梯附近，请勿停留，以防堵塞。

44. Tender grass needs your care.
    柔弱的小草需要你的呵护。

45. Hotel is not responsible for articles lost or stolen.
    遗失物品，酒店概不负责。

46. Please do not panic if the hotel is on fire.
    如果饭店发生火灾，请不要惊慌。

47. Don't smoke in bed, or the ashes fallen to the ground may be yourself.
    请勿在床上吸烟，否则落地的灰烬可能就是你自己。

48. Distinguished guest: Please sing songs in your heart, as our walls are not as thick as you may imagine.

    尊敬的客人，请把您的歌藏在心里，因为我们的墙壁并没有您想象得那么厚实。

49. Put towels you want washed on the floor. Leave towels you will use again on the towel racks. This simple gesture helps protect the environment. Thank you.

    将您需要清洗的毛巾放在地板上，将您准备继续使用的毛巾挂在毛巾架上。您的举手之劳将有助环保。谢谢！

参考文献

[1] 胡扬政. 酒店英语服务实训 [M]. 北京：清华大学出版社，2008.
[2] 肖璇. 现代酒店英语实务教程 [M]. 北京：世界图书出版公司，2006.
[3] 雷兵. 酒店英语听说实训教程 [M]. 北京：科学出版社，2009.
[4] 郭兆康. 饭店情景英语 [M]. 上海：复旦大学出版社，2016.
[5] 本书编写组. 饭店工作英语 [M]. 北京：中国旅游出版社，2002.
[6] 柯淑萍，孙培. 饭店英语听说教程 [M]. 杭州：浙江大学出版社，2008.
[7] 张伟. 饭店英语 [M]. 天津：南开大学出版社，2005.
[8] 李佳. 饭店英语 [M]. 2版. 北京：化学工业出版社，2014.
[9] 梁文霞，董宁函. 酒店饭店英语口语 [M]. 大连：大连理工大学出版社，2015.
[10] 许雪敏，邢怡. 饭店英语视听说 [M]. 上海：上海交通大学出版社，2015.
[11] 张丽君. 酒店英语 [M]. 2版. 北京：清华大学出版社，2018.
[12] 朱华. 酒店英语（视听版）[M]. 2版. 北京：北京大学出版社，2021.
[13] 韩雪. 酒店英语听说强化教程 [M]. 4版. 北京：旅游教育出版社，2021.